Education
in a Free Society

Education
in a Free Society

Anne Husted Burleigh, Editor

Liberty Fund

Indianapolis

This book is published by Liberty Fund, Inc., a foundation established to encourage study of the ideal of a society of free and responsible individuals.

The cuneiform inscription that serves as the design motif for our endpapers is the earliest-known written appearance of the word "freedom" (*amagi*), or "liberty." It is taken from a clay document written about 2300 B.C. in the Sumerian city-state of Lagash.

Library of Congress Cataloging in Publication Data

Burleigh, Anne Husted, ed., 1941–
  Education in a free society.

  1. Education, Higher—Aims and objectives—Congresses.
  I. Burleigh, Anne Husted, 1941–   ed.   II. Liberty Fund.
LB2301.E38   378.´01   73-78807
ISBN 0-913966-45-2

05 04 03 02 01 C 7 6 5 4 3
04 03 02 01 96 P   6 5 4 3 2

Contents

ESSAY FIVE

Foreword

Liberty Fund, Inc., was established to encourage study of the ideal of a society of free and responsible individuals who are free from intimidation. This ideal (not utopian) is the polestar by which the directors make their decisions.

In carrying out its purposes, Liberty Fund has made grants to organizations with similar objectives, assisted in special projects and in the writing and publication of ideas involving education conducive to a society of free and responsible people, and organized and sponsored seminars.

The seminars organized by Liberty Fund take their format from the Socratic seminar. The material to be discussed is read by the participants prior to the seminar. The discussion group is kept small to promote a maximum exchange of ideas. The leader asks a minimum of questions but mainly polices the discussion so that as much participation as possible may occur.

Liberty Fund proceeds upon the premise that if we are going to have a society of free and responsible people, they must have some capacity to read and write and reason. How can those capacities best be developed in a free society? What would be the ideal educational arrangement in human society and, in particular, in a society of free and responsible human beings?

In an effort to explore these questions two of Liberty Fund's directors, B. A. Rogge and P. F. Goodrich, collaborated in writing a position paper, "Education in a Free Society," in which they attempted to set forth the problems. Four well-known writers and educators (Gottfried Dietze, Russell Kirk, Henry Manne, and Stephen Tonsor) were asked to present papers dealing with this subject to a seminar which was held in Indianapolis March 28–31, 1971.

The field of expertise of these men was in the college and university; therefore, this seminar dealt primarily with that level of education. However, Dorothy Sayers' "The Lost Tools of Learning" was inserted as background material concerning primary and secondary education.

Participants in this seminar other than paperwriters were Paul L. Adams, Dean of Hillsdale College; Anne Husted Burleigh, writer; Jameson G. Campaigne, Editorial Writer of the New York *Daily News;* John Chamberlain, columnist and Dean of the School of Journalism of Troy State University; William H. Fletcher, Partner, Arthur Andersen & Co.; Robert G. Jones, Principal,

Winchester (Indiana) Community High School; Israel
M. Kirzner, Professor of Economics, New York University; George C. Roche, President of Hillsdale College; Arthur A. Shenfield, International Institute for
Economic Research; Randall Storms, Headmaster,
Wichita Collegiate School; Linda Haifley Walker, public school teacher. These participants have wide audi-
ences in their regular vocations. There were also
observers present who did not participate in the discussion.

Anne Husted Burleigh has summarized the discussion in the introduction to this book, entitled "Education Seminar."

In a time of turmoil in public education, it is felt that
these writers have ideas that, in a free market, could
develop into something highly worthwhile, even though
we may not at this moment be able to predict what form
that might take. Thus, Liberty Fund presents its ideas to
the public with the hope that some little seed will take
hold and help bring us closer to the ideal of a society
of free and responsible people.

Education
in a Free Society

Introduction

Education Seminar

Anne Husted Burleigh

Anne Husted Burleigh received a B.A. with honors in history from DePauw University in 1963 and did graduate work at Indiana University in 1963–64. She is the author of John Adams, *a historical biography published in 1969, and has written articles and reviews for such publications as* Intercollegiate Review, Analysis, *and* Academic Reviewer. *She is a former staff reporter for* The Indianapolis Star.

No other institution plays a more central role in the life of the American family than the public school. Perhaps even more than the church the public school provides the context in which people make the major decisions of their lives.

There are more public schools today than ever before in our history; more students than ever attend the public schools. But scarcely anyone today is happy with the public schools in the United States, whether those institutions be of kindergarten or university level. Hardly anyone would deny that the gravest problems riddle the public school system, that even as more schools are built and more tax money is rushed in to salve the wounds, the dilemma persists and intensifies.

If it were possible, many may wonder, to pry loose from the present educational system, to start afresh with a system of any choosing, what sort of educational arrangements would we make? What arrangements would coincide with the nature of man, his search for freedom, his quest for understanding of the spiritual and physical world? What role would the state have in these arrangements? Is there an alternative to state provision and compulsion of education? Even if the state were not to subsidize education, is education so necessary to a free citizenry that the state at least ought to compel people to send their children to school? If we could answer those questions, then we might know in what direction to head in trying to extricate ourselves from the present educational predicament.

And so, to explore a scheme of education that they would consider ideal, a group of scholars brought together by the Liberty Fund, Inc., met March 28–31, 1971. Since the participants in the seminar were proponents of limited government and a free market, their intent was to examine the ideal educational arrangements in a society of free and responsible people. How the citizens of a free society should provide for education of their children and what should be the composition of that framework was the subject designated in advance as the topic for investigation.

A position paper, "Education in a Free Society," the work of Pierre F. Goodrich and Dr. Benjamin A. Rogge, served as a springboard for discussion. Hence, a summary of the position paper must precede the report of the seminar proceedings.

The Position Paper

When the authors speak in their paper of ideal educational arrangements, they do not have in mind a system suitable for a paradise inhabited by perfectible beings. Instead, they consider the optimal framework for educating a society of imperfect human beings—intellectually, morally, spiritually imperfect—who, though improvable, cannot in this life escape their condition. The authors, though accepting the idea that perfection exists, think that imperfect men can never know perfection but can hope only to know the optimal —and probably not even that. In other words, men who put their imperfect minds to the task of pursuing perfection will do well to discover merely the optimal answer; viewing the world through myopic eyes, they will perceive only half-truths, partial truths. Nonetheless, they must make choices, and so with their hazy, constricted perception of the ideal, they will try to make the best of imperfect choices. In the context of the position paper, then, ideal is assumed to be optimal— that is, the closest approximation to perfection that imperfect men can conceive.

Since men are imperfect, they consequently have need of improvement; they require education to acquire the vestments of civilization. Education, as defined by the authors, is growth in understanding on the part of a particular human being. It is an interior process for the individual and can happen anywhere, not just in the classroom or school. Furthermore, because of the infinite variety of human beings, because of their diverse capabilities and inclinations, no one kind of education suits them all equally well. Thus, the ideal educational arrangements will allow for these wide variances. In their definition of education, the authors are quick to point out that education will not transform man into God. Though it may be hoped that education will turn man down the path toward virtue, it will not necessarily do so; education will not make man perfect.

With "ideal" and "education" thus described, the position paper defines the free society as one in which each individual is free to do anything that is peaceful, where he is free to behave responsibly and free from intimidation. In other words, the free society is one in which the state serves only as night watchman.

After this brief introduction, the authors pose three problems: First of all, What are the purposes of education in a free society? Second, What economic and political arrangements will be most harmonious with those purposes? And, finally, What kinds of educational techniques will most likely meet those purposes?

Because it is assumed that the purpose of education in an unfree society will be to serve the whim of the dictator, proletariat, priest-king, or whoever holds power, the authors are concerned only with the purposes of education in a society of free and responsible men.* They believe that in a state where government acts only to prevent people from harming each other the answer to the problem of the purpose of education will be a simple one. The state will have no purpose of education at all. Rather, education, as are all endeavors other than police action, will be totally a matter of individual concern. Only the individual in a free society will define the purpose of education. Whether he wants to become the classically educated Renaissance man or to become the best barber in town is entirely up to him. The choice of what he will do with his education belongs only to him. So long as he does only that which is peaceful, he has sole control over the means and ends of his actions.

For that reason, the authors of the position paper argue that all intervention by the state in the educational process is both unnecessary and undesirable. Except as the state protects its citizens against force and fraud, it will have no authority in any aspect of the educational picture. The authors make an unqualified statement in this regard:

> We oppose state operation of educational programs at any level; we oppose state finance of such programs at any

---

* The authors are concerned about the question of what is to become of those people who are either internal or external enemies of the free society, who are incapable of exercising freedom or who are unwilling to exercise it. The authors, however, do not deal with these issues in their position paper.

level, in any form (including tax relief); we oppose state coercion or participation in such programs, whether public or private. We believe that education must, by its nature, be a part of the *private* sector of society. . . .

But at this point arises the inevitable question: Can the citizens of a free society be assumed to make the choices that will preserve their freedom or must they be educated specifically in the principles of freedom? Burdened by their imperfections, may they not likely succumb to the temptation of short-term benefits that the unfree society offers? If so, then should they deliberately be educated to opt for freedom? Should the state compel education of its citizens in the institutions of a free society?

"In other words," ask the authors of the position paper, "does the survival of the free society require that its citizens be unfree in at least the one area of education?" As the authors point out, most societies that have described themselves as free have always refused to trust the citizen to exercise complete freedom in the field of education. By compulsory school attendance laws, tax support of schools in whole or in part, and authority over curriculum, most states throughout history have used their coercive power to regulate education. All such interventions of the state are both unnecessary and undesirable, say the authors. If the citizens wish to make sure that their children are educated for freedom, then they will see that society as a political unit is excluded from all decisions concerning

education, except as the state protects people from force
and fraud. The authors believe that history has revealed
too often how dismal are the results when corruptible
men, lusting for power as all men do, use state control
of education to enhance the power of the state and of
themselves. The authors insist that "the task of educating individuals for freedom, if done at all, will be best
done by private agencies and institutions, manned by
individuals deeply committed to that cause." Some
private agencies within the free society no doubt will
preach a philosophy antithetical to freedom. Nor can
people be expected to be attracted automatically to the
structures of a free society. Nonetheless, this is a small
risk when contrasted with the danger of state control
in which the state in all probability would *not* teach its
citizens to limit its power. It is simply inherent in the
state that it will refuse to retreat from any extension
of power to which it can force itself. (Also see Thomas
Hobbes, *Leviathan.*)

If, then, educational arrangements are to be made
wholly by individuals and not at all by the state, a
further problem arises when the individual who is the
educational subject is a child rather than an adult
competent to make decisions. In such a case, who is
responsible for the child—parent, voluntary welfare
agency, state? The authors of the position paper are
firm in their insistence upon parental responsibility for
education. Imperfect as some parents may be, the state
may claim no jurisdiction over the parent-child relation-

ship (except, again, in cases of force). The family, the authors say, though imperfect, is still the least imperfect decision-maker for its children—and is a far less imperfect decision-maker than the state. Those who make decisions should be ideally those who bear the consequences, hence making parents or guardians peculiarly suited to judging the educational interests of their children until those children become financially independent and responsible for themselves.

Thus, either the individual directly involved or the person legally responsible for him is the proper one to decide the purpose of education in a free society. Much as the authors of the position paper would like to see everyone educated in the ideal of a free society, they refuse to take the risk of state intervention in that education. They prefer instead "the uncertain outcome of competitive educational programs, free of state control."

Affirming that individuals will be able to decide for themselves why and in what way they will be educated, the authors next tackle the economic and political arrangements in which these individual purposes may be carried out. Politically the free society will be, as already stated, a limited state with government restricted to being a night watchman with authority only in cases of force and fraud.

"We begin," say the authors, "by assuming a society in which the state plays no part in the educational process. Gone would be all state colleges and universities, all public elementary and secondary schools, all public libraries and public opera houses. . . ." What, then, will be the economic arrangement for education in a free society? With all publicly supported institutions absent, what would take their place? The authors cannot certainly predict. Without actually trying a free society, no one will ever know what manifold choices it offers. The private sector of education as it exists today suffers from such a clutter of state interventions that it gives no good clue to the answer. Nonetheless, the private sector in other endeavors is relatively free enough to indicate some possibilities for really private education.

In the first place, great diversity would be likely in the kinds of educational opportunity. Books, tapes, newspapers, films, televised lectures, and so forth, might be more utilized than at present—all much less expensive than traditional methods of formal teacher and textbook. Second, more schools might be operated on a profit basis, in contrast to the less efficient not-for-profit institutions now prevalent. Finally, the formal schools that would exist in a free society would be at least as varied as those that now function in the private sector. Some schools might stress liberal arts, others vocational studies; some would be religiously affiliated, others secular; some would cater to gifted students, others to handicapped, still others to minority groups, to wealthy students or poor ones. Some schools would be highly structured; others might be no more than meetings held in someone's home. In other words, the schools of a free society would be strictly consumer-oriented.

The authors of the position paper next ask: "How should education be financed—how should it be priced and whose funds should be used to pay that price?" Traditionally, in their opinion, education has been regarded as different from other goods, hence subject to different financial arrangements and subject to the yoke of state control. For two reasons education has been seen as unique: first, because of a spillover of benefits from the educated individual to all of society; second, because of enhanced career opportunities attained through education, thus supposedly making necessary some kind of equal educational opportunity for all.

The authors object to the spillover argument. They believe it condones forcing one person through educational taxes to give up his power to decide what will benefit him in the area of education and instead to pay for another's education, whether or not he regards someone else's education as a worthy object on which to spend his money. Likewise the authors reject the equal opportunity argument. Human beings are so diverse in interest, talents, character and ability that no similarity of opportunity will ever make them equal. Consequently, the only equality that can exist—and must exist—in a free society is equality before the law. Coercion marks all other forms of equality.

Though modern parlance often casts education as a *right,* education cannot be so regarded if it is true to the classical conception: a right is an inherent and just claim that the owner expects others to respect and that, likewise, must be respected in others. The natural rights doctrine of the seventeenth, eighteenth and nineteenth centuries defined a triad of rights: life, liberty and property.* According to John Locke, with whom the authors of the position paper agree, the right to own property is a natural right, but no one has a right to other people's property. Everyone has a right to seek his education in any way that is peaceful, without coercion from anyone else. He does not, however, have the right to take another's property to attain that education. Consequently, the authors do not recognize any right of one man to another's property for purposes of education. They conclude that "the concept that all must be assured of some form of education, regardless of desire or financial ability, is thus rejected in principle." Moreover, they question the argument that schooling is essential to opportunity. They suspect that much of the apparent higher income due to increased schooling is often a result of state requirements for college degrees as passports to certain professions.

The authors find other arguments against the current method of financing education through public subsidy. First, such below-cost pricing fosters glaring inefficiencies in management that in a competitive, private sys-

---

* Locke also spoke of ". . . lives, liberties and estates, which I call by the general name 'property.' . . ."

tem would be weeded out. Second, the current method fails to sort out those students who do not care to be in school and have no intention of trying to learn. If schools were private, only those students with high motivation would care enough to pay the full price of education; those who did not care for formal schooling would be free to find some other pursuit in keeping with their taste and abilities. Finally, when teachers are not awarded salaries commensurate with their talents, when they are given fixed salaries regardless of how hard they work, when they report not to the parents of their students but to the state government, then they, too, lack motivation. A private system in which parents pay teachers for a commodity—education—should produce excellence in both quality of teachers and the product they offer.

"In summary, then," say the authors, *"tax-supported education tends to make of our schools and colleges a collection of nonstudents under the tutelage of non-teachers and the administration of the incompetent."* The authors reject the view that education should be treated as a special case; instead, they believe it should be regarded as a commodity in competition with all other goods and services in the marketplace, subject only to rules against fraud. Although they cannot pretend to say what kinds of educational enterprises would emerge in a free society, the authors do expect a mixture of for-profit and not-for-profit institutions, with for-profit institutions setting the economic pace. Furthermore, they would expect teachers and administrations to be fully responsive to the interests of students and parents. With students paying the full cost of their education, institutions would rise or fall upon student support. Because demand for their services would determine teacher salaries, the tenure system would vanish. The authors are convinced that competent teachers do not require tenure; they believe, moreover, that the frequent argument of academic freedom holds no weight:

> We do believe in the ideal that each man should be free to say what he will, but we don't believe that any one of us has the right to say what he will—and be paid for the saying of it by someone else who doesn't wish to so pay us! In this sense, academic freedom is, in fact, a denial of freedom—the freedom of each man to expend his resources on only those uses that he sees fit—including the choice of sources of learning.

The authors insist that a truly private educational system, rather than a public one, *"would surely provide more and better educational opportunities at a far lower cost per unit of delivered product (i.e., per unit growth in knowledge) than the current system."* The answer to the financing of education, they think, is to let each family, using either its own funds or those willingly donated by others, pay for the education of its children in any manner it sees fit, "whether that which is purchased be a book, a television set or four years at Harvard College."

In the last section of the position paper, the authors

describe their ideal college. They make clear that in a free educational marketplace others might not choose this ideal as their ideal; there would be no power, of course, to constrain others to choose the ideal of the authors.

For the authors, the ideal college is one in which it is likely that those students who attend will become not only committed to the free society but knowledgeable of its principles and the evils against which it contends. They hope that their college would produce converts who are understanding and rational, not simply ones who are responding to emotional appeal.

To the possible argument that the authors propose a propaganda mechanism, rather than an educational program, they reply with two rebuttals. First, since it is impossible for teachers to be completely objective, all educational institutions, whether their administrators admit it or not, have a planned or unplanned point of view. The authors would state openly and honestly the point of view of their school so that students and their parents would find no surprises. Second, the authors assert that any sufficiently intelligent person, upon reflection and some genuine study of human experience, will see the value of a free society of responsible men living under the rule of law. In other words, even though people may be beguiled in another direction, they have some kind of natural inclination toward freedom.

The authors, knowing that they are more familiar

with college education than with lower levels, have restricted their discussion to the university level. They support, however, application of the same principles to elementary education. They have restricted themselves, in addition, to the liberal arts college. Having no objection to vocational and professional training, they nonetheless think that study of the liberal arts not only will afford the best understanding of the questions of freedom but also will increase the competence of people in their given vocations.

As to the structure of the ideal college, the authors require its ownership to be private, with control residing in a specified person or group. Though it could be either for-profit or not-for-profit, the authors would prefer for-profit. Decisions of policy would be made by a board of trustees and executed by an administration.

The authors would outline their personnel policies and practices in the following way: Faculty members would be selected for their qualities as teachers. Most would be deeply committed to the philosophy of the free society. Because the authors believe that the outcome of true learning will be such a commitment, they would think it inconsistent to search for true scholars among those not so committed. Yet, given human fallibility, the authors hesitate to claim a corner on the truth; for that reason and for the peculiar student rejection of what seem to be loaded dice, they would not object to including a few faculty members who criticize the free society.

Faculty members would serve at the pleasure of the administration. Their income would depend upon their effectiveness as teachers. Or perhaps the students, after paying basic fees to the college to handle overhead expenses, would pay most of teacher salaries in the form of fees.

The curriculum of the college would be presented through three vehicles—individual study by students, seminars on assigned readings, and faculty lectures. With the help of counselors or members of the faculty, students could choose their areas of study. Their obligation would be simply to behave properly and to read the assigned material. But they would be encouraged to read additional works from a list of the world's great literature. Because their term of study would depend upon their own interest, if they behaved correctly, they could attend for as long as they liked. No degrees or diplomas would be granted, however. The authors consider degrees meaningless. Nor would teachers and fields of knowledge be divided into departments. Though the faculty, of course, would be of diversified specialties, the authors would avoid artificial departmental lines.

Students would pursue their studies, first, through reading; then through Socratic discussion under trained leadership; and, finally, through faculty lectures. The authors list these methods according to both importance and chronology. Though there would be no grades, students could write papers or examinations, if they wanted, for evaluation. In return for this evaluation, they would pay the faculty members additional fees. The authors favor a no-grade system, "not because we are opposed to competition for excellence among students, but because the real purpose of education is for each individual to make the maximum progress possible *for that person*—and for this, relative judgments are not significant."

There would be no entrance requirements except the necessary funds to pay, garnered either from the students themselves or from voluntary donors.

There would be no responsibility at this college for the private lives of the students. Other schools in the free society might serve *in loco parentis,* but this one would not.

The authors argue in their paper "that the educational arrangements currently in use in this country are grossly inefficient, inequitable, contrary to human rights, contrary to human nature and destructive of the society of free and responsible men." The alternative they offer is a strictly private system, subject to the rules of the marketplace and free from state control. Only such an arrangement, they believe, can produce individuals educated in and committed to the philosophy of a society of free and responsible people.

"It seems unlikely," the authors concede, "that the American society will move rapidly (if at all) in the directions we have indicated. But this we do know: if there are none in the society who stand ready to hold out the ideal of a more hopeful arrangement, real progress is not only unlikely—it is forever impossible."

The Discussion

With the position paper as a focal point, and looking toward a more hopeful educational arrangement than the present system, the participants in the seminar wrestled with a blueprint for an ideal framework. The issues of the discussion divided into two segments: first, the principle or goal of the university in a free society and, second, the accomplishment of the goal. (The seminar, although including thoughts on arrangements for education of young children in the general picture of education in a free society, devoted itself most specifically to the subject of university education.)

Within the discussion of the goal of the university there were three points of consideration—definition of a free society, definition of education and exposition of the purpose of the university. In the discussion of how the goal of the university would be accomplished, a number of questions arose: Will the university be controlled in any way by the state? Who will own the university? How will it be administered? How will it be financed? Who will attend it? What will be its curriculum and method of educating?

When the participants set about discussing the principle or goal of the university in a free society, they ran into the immediate problem of the definition of a free society. Despite the idea of the state as night watchman having been a keystone of the position paper, that notion of the state was subject to various interpretations. One participant, at least, declared that he could not speak in terms of the ideal free society, that a truly free society would amount to Rousseau's state of nature. Construing a free society to be one without government, this participant stated that limited government is not by definition a free society. Another member rejoined that an ideal free society, as the authors of the position paper had meant it, was limited government, a night-watchman state. To go beyond that, he said, to have no government would be anarchy, a tyranny of each by all, an unfree society.

In this same vein of discussion there were conflicting definitions of freedom. On the one hand, some defined freedom as the absence of coercion; on the other hand, Dr. Henry Manne spoke of it as the power to do something. Some participants objected to Dr. Manne's statement on the grounds that confusion of freedom with ability makes discussion virtually impossible, that freedom cannot be defined other than as absence of coercion. Dr. Manne then clarified his definition of freedom as the ability of an individual to maximize his own utility, to make effective choices. Dr. Israel Kirzner, suggesting that Dr. Manne defined freedom as the absence of obstacles to achievement of desires, offered a description of freedom as the absence of interference from others in the exercise of rights to which one is entitled. None of the participants referred to the definition of freedom offered in the position paper —the right to do anything that is peaceful. This definition is similar to Dr. Kirzner's view of freedom as the right to do anything one wishes to do, so long as it does not interfere with the rights of others.

The final problem in defining a free society was the difficulty encountered by the participants in talking in terms of an ideal, an optional society of free and responsible men. Instead, they strayed into discussions of the practical world as it is and of the problems that they confront in their various educational institutions.

When the discussion focused on the definition of education, the participants first examined the premise of the position paper that men are and always will be imperfect. Although some participants strove to base that assumption on a belief in God, others preferred not to mount that proposition in theology, a proposition that they thought would have equal validity and broader appeal if it were not a theological one. At any rate, the imperfectibility of man received no rebuttals. To the question of how the conclusions of the position paper depended upon the imperfection of man, it was answered that whether one accepted a man's imperfection or whether he considered man perfectible would determine the structure of society toward which he would incline. If some men are perfect, then it would be logical for them to coerce others, a notion that breeds totalitarianism. Moreover, the very notion of educability assumes that men are imperfect, one participant asserted. If they are perfect, then they have no need of education.

The definition of education proposed in the position paper—a growth in understanding for a particular human being—came under fire by some participants. Understanding what, they asked. Understanding man and his universe or understanding something else? Dr. Gottfried Dietze objected to elaboration of the word understanding, which he thought would confine the term education within too narrow boundaries.

The late Dorothy Sayers, in a paper used as background material for the seminar, "The Lost Tools of Learning," defined the "sole true end of education" as simply "to teach men how to learn for themselves." The Sayers paper, which pressed for teaching young children the tools of learning embodied in the medieval trivium of grammar, dialectic and rhetoric, received unanimous acclaim among the participants.

The end of education was described in another fashion by Dr. Russell Kirk, seminar participant and author of "The Revitalized College: A Model," a paper used as background material. Dr. Kirk called the chief end of a college of arts and sciences "to enable a body of senior scholars (the professors) and a body of junior scholars (the undergraduates) to seek after wisdom— and, through wisdom, for truth." A headful of facts, practical training, "or even knowledge" does not constitute wisdom. Wisdom means "apprehension of the human condition, recognition of reality, and the experience and possession of high knowledge—together with the power to apply experience and knowledge critically and practically." To support his concept of wisdom, Dr. Kirk quoted John Henry Newman, to whom the real aim of education was knowledge acted upon by reason: "the clear, calm, accurate vision and comprehension of all things, as far as the finite mind can embrace them, each in its own place, and with its own characteristics upon it." Though Dr. Kirk declared in his paper that the college could, in a formal sense, do only a small bit toward conferring this "wise vision," he affirmed that if it could at least help to instill this vision, then it would have "done much to enable a man to order his own soul, and thereby come to a condition of moral worth." The term "moral worth" was never explicitly defined, but it may be assumed that Dr. Kirk meant "moral worth" when he wrote of "an apprehension of what man is and wherein his duties lie and in what his dignity consists." Not only was the idea of the college imparting a sense of moral worth crucial to his paper, but it occasioned a debate on the ethical neutrality of the university that was one of the high points of the seminar. Should the university be ethically uncommitted, the participants questioned. Is it even possible to be ethically uncommitted?

As part of that discussion, the participants asked Dr. Kirk what he meant when he said in his paper that

"the higher learning is an intellectual means to an
ethical end; that the college is meant to join knowledge
with virtue." If, as both Newman and Kirk emphasized,
the aim of formal learning is cultivation of the intellect
for the intellect's own sake, then the participants
puzzled over Dr. Kirk's statement that "the means must
be strictly and rigorously intellectual" but "the end
must be ethical, in that right reason is employed to
attain moral worth." The relationship of the unhamp-
ered pursuit of truth in the university to the attempted
inculcation of virtue in the students was never un-
tangled by the participants. Agreeing with Dr. Kirk
that virtue cannot be taught formally through indoctrination, that it is attained indirectly and subtly, some,
nonetheless, were skeptical of his assumption that the
wise man who understands the moral principles in
human nature is likely to be virtuous. Though a man
may understand the truth, the participants thought, it
does not necessarily follow that he will conform his
will to the truth in order to act virtuously. Dr. Kirk,
however, stressed throughout the discussion the importance of intellectual *means* to an ethical end. When
one participant, defining virtue as right action moti-
vated by right will and guided by right reason, inquired
whether Dr. Kirk would say that the role of the university was with right reason rather than with right
will, Dr. Kirk replied that the role of the university was
to order the reason. Another participant, in an effort
to summarize the issue, cautioned against confusing

two kinds of morality, the morality of right conduct and the intellectual morality taught in the university; the code of intellectual morality must be to pursue truth even though the truth may destroy the seeker.

An essential question arose at this point: Must the university be ethically neutral, or may the university, devoted to the pursuit of truth, rightfully take a stand in favor of the free society? Several participants answered that a college catalog may properly state, but not as an official university policy, that some of its faculty, in the honest pursuit of truth, believe the general welfare to be optimally promoted by a free society.

Absolute ethical neutrality is impossible, the participants agreed. Regardless of every effort that the true scholar will make toward objectivity, his limited human capacities render him short of his mark each time. Because he is a human rather than a divine scholar, he begins his pursuit of truth at some level below absolute objectivity. Consequently, the point at which he starts makes a difference. As one participant pointed out, there is, for example, no *Christian* history, no *Christian* economics; but the Christian looking at history or economics will see it from a perspective different from that of the secularist or the Marxist.

That the scholar will certainly fail to discover the full truth, however, does not detain him from striving to find it. In so doing, he may uncover partial truth; perhaps his imperfect knowledge will be part of a perfect whole. Hence, all participants agreed, the purpose of the university must be to allow the pursuit of truth. Or, as one participant corrected, the pursuit of truth should be the aim not of the collective body of the university but of the individuals within the university.

Although everyone admitted to the crucial place of the pursuit of truth, several of the group were unwilling to place the formalized pursuit of truth in the form of research as the most important function of the university. This reluctance spurred a key debate, chiefly between Dr. Stephen Tonsor and Dr. Dietze, on whether teaching or research should have top priority in the university. Though every scholar is a researcher and is devoted to the pursuit of truth for its own sake, Dr. Tonsor asserted, the pursuit of truth through formal research should take second place to teaching. The primary function of a university, he thought, is the transmission and augmentation of a cultural tradition.

"What the university or the college does is give the student those skills and abilities which will enable him to avail himself of all of the goods, both technical and spiritual, which inhere in our particular cultural tradition," Dr. Tonsor emphasized. Expressing a more European view, Dr. Dietze stated that research in the university should have priority over teaching, that in the university the scholar searches for truth and only secondarily shares his insights with his students. When teaching gains ascendance, Dr. Dietze stated, the preference of the institution is to let students know the state of the truth as it is presumed at present. On the other hand, when research is foremost, the interest of the school is in having the truth further pursued.

To both sides of this debate, Dr. Kirzner protested that both Tonsor and Dietze treated the university as an autonomous entity with a function of its own. In the free society, he said, universities would emerge in response to various demands of consumers. It might be, for instance, that economy would require that research and teaching be carried on in the same institution. Since education would be a commodity in the marketplace, each institution would resolve its own question of priority of research or teaching. Consumers then would decide whether they preferred to send their children to a school emphasizing research or teaching or both.

Dr. Kirzner's objection revealed a basic difference among the participants over whether the university is simply an enterprise offering a product for sale or whether it is a community of scholars with a life of its own. If the university is a business enterprise, then it consists of a contractual relationship between the trustees and the students. On the other hand, if the university is a community with a life of its own, then it is the sort of organism around which revolves the political theory of the organic state.

Those in the seminar who thought of the university as nothing more than a contract binding it to its students spoke of the university as having no absolute right to existence. They questioned Dr. Dietze on his paper, "Reason of University," in which, they believed, he expounded an organic concept of the university. One participant protested the analogy that Dr. Dietze had drawn between the state and the university because it suggested a mystical or collectivist idea about the university. In his paper, however, Dr. Dietze wrote that "universities are not organisms into which their members are born and from childhood on adjusted to certain ways of thinking and living. They are institutions that may have grown organically but are, nevertheless, based upon a contract freely concluded among thinking individuals conferring rights and duties upon the contracting partners." Adhering to the notion of the university as a contractual relationship, Dr. Dietze at the same time expanded the idea of the university to the medieval concept of a community of scholars, making it more than simply a private institution. In his view, though the university is not a separate living being, the members within would surely be united in common bond and purpose. By such a presentation, he sought to satisfy modern critics of the university who see the university as an organism.

For Dr. Dietze the function of the university must be the pursuit of truth. Truth, he said, is the apex of all values, the only value about which there is no doubt; thus, in a sense, it is value-free. Because the university alone among human institutions exists specifically to pursue truth and the pursuit of truth is essential, he emphasized, then the university is essential. Because truth may be pursued only in freedom, then universities ideally are bastions of liberalism. If we live in a totalitarian century, as Dr. Dietze is convinced, the preservation of the university is more crucial than ever. In this authoritarian age, he declared, universities stand as islands of libertarianism, of the free pursuit of learning. To defend the university, then, against those inside or outside of it who would destroy it as a haven in which to seek truth, he proposed in his paper "reason of university"—that is, what the university can and should do to preserve itself as an institution for the pursuit of truth.

In possibly the most heated discussion of the seminar, Dr. Dietze's opponents countered that he was not presenting his proposal as a plan for the university in a free society but for the university as a refuge, an island of freedom within a totalitarian society. Yet in a free society, they declared, a university is no more than any institution, with no absolute right to exist. A university, they believed, should rise or fall on its own merits, without recourse to reason of university. Dr. Dietze, in arguing for the right of the university to defend itself, said he hoped through the preservation of the university to turn from the present controlled society to a free society. He noted that universities had been highly important in the creation of the free society of the nineteenth century.

When the discussion turned from the principle of the goal of the university in the free society to how this goal should be accomplished, the participants confronted the basic question: Will the university be controlled in any way by the state? Many participants agreed that education is a scarce economic good to be allocated, that it is best handled by the competition of the market alone. Yet, at the same time, the question of whether the free society could exist without citizens educated in its principles was a matter of common concern. If that society could not exist without an educated citizenry, should the state provide that education? Further, should it compel that education? Most participants supported the position paper in answering no to those questions. But both Dr. Dietze and Dr. Kirk, though making clear that they much preferred private to public institutions, said that they would accept public institutions if, in the free society, private ones failed to emerge. As Dr. Dietze put it, he believes in the liberal principle, but to save that liberal principle for the long run he would, if necessary, vote to tax others to support his university. Dr. Kirk, in particular, worried that the traditional classical values of education might vanish in a free society if put to the market vote of a democratic populace. He believed the finest traditions of our cultural heritage to be at stake. Consequently, he hesitated to put them at the mercy of consumers who, he thought, would be likely to choose the lowest common denominator.

Dr. George Roche replied that even though we cannot be sure whether or not some traditional educational values might be altered or destroyed in the free society, there is good evidence that they would survive. On the other hand, he said, it is sure that in a "modern, majoritarian, egalitarian, politicalized society" the traditional values would not survive. "Education," Dr. Roche pointed out, "presumably rests upon the individual and improving the quality of his choices and the quality of his life, and Leviathan doesn't like individuals." Another participant, while acknowledging that the free society could not survive without education, maintained that it did not follow that the state must have anything to do with the production of education. It does not have to subsidize or provide that education. Even if, by some unlikely chance, no educational arrangements appeared in the market, it would be immoral for the state to provide them. That chance, however, he deemed remote, remarking that it was more likely that the diversity of educational opportunities offered would accommodate far more people than does the present system.

To the question of whether we can be certain that in a free society there would be a development of intelligence, of an understanding of the free society to make it possible for that society to continue, most participants supported the position paper in saying that though they could not be certain, they were willing to take a chance on the free market. Most were convinced that government provision and compulsion of education would destroy the free society.

Who will own the university in a free society? Though most participants followed the position paper in naming a lay board of trustees, they were receptive to Dr. Manne's proposal, expressed in his paper, "The Political Economy of Modern Universities," for a unique faculty ownership through transferable shares of stock in the university. Designed to solve what some described as a deplorable lack of interest among the trustees of modern universities, Dr. Manne's suggestion, as he put it, would recognize de jure what already exists de facto—that the faculties now own the universities, that they have moved into the power vacuum left by impotent trustees. If the faculty could obtain shares of stock, Dr. Manne claimed, the university in another generation or so would be run as a corporation on a for-profit basis.

As to the problem of how the university should be administered, most participants accepted the traditional plan of trustees' authority exercised through a president. Dr. Tonsor in his paper, "Authority, Power, and the University," offered a proposal intended to end the practice of trustees' "rubber-stamping administration decisions without sufficient examination" of the background of those decisions. Dr. Tonsor would allow the governing board of trustees to have a secretary independent of the administration, whose job would be to investigate "administrative proposals, budgets and appointments." This secretary "would provide the necessary extramural expertise which alone can insure that the decisions of the administration fall into line with the policy of the governing board." Such a fact-finder would go a long way, Dr. Tonsor hoped, toward making the trustees responsible, toward renewing them in their task of holding in trust the authority of the university.

A different twist to solution of the difficulty of administration was proposed by Dr. Kirk in the form of a faculty senate, which would manage academic affairs. This senate would choose from staff members college deans to handle administrative details. The president of the school would be chosen by the trustees from a group of nominees put up by the senate. It was not clear how the members of the academic senate would be selected. Dr. Kirk did insist, however, that the senate would operate under a limited constitution. The plan of a faculty senate met with little favor among the participants, some of whom questioned in particular the ability of such a body to deal with personnel problems of the university. One participant pointed out at this point that in a free market it would be likely that much of the organizational hierarchy of which the group complained would simply pass away. In a free society, he said, the property owner could delegate responsibility to anyone he chose. Consequently, the issue of whether control should reside in a board of trustees or a faculty senate would not be crucial. Since schools embodying both types of control would doubtless emerge in the market, the consumers could suit themselves.

Further, the participants disagreed extensively on the question of tenure. Though some supported the position paper in its rejection of tenure as a denial of the freedom of the trustees to use their resources as they saw fit, others were just as firm that tenure was necessary to preserve the intellectual integrity of the scholar, just as tenure preserves a judge in his independence.

On the issue of how the university should be financed, the participants agreed upon the principle of full-cost tuition, with the exception of Dr. Kirk, whose model college included a significant endowment. In conjunction with the position paper, some participants disallowed not only endowments but also tax exemptions, which, as described by Dr. Manne in his paper, are "nothing more than indirect subsidies by government to private educational institutions, and there is no apparent justification for this reallocation of taxpayers' wealth." One participant summarized his distrust of so-called untied dollars by saying that there was no such thing as a free lunch, a free endowment dollar or a free tax dollar.

Most participants endorsed the for-profit institution. Because the criteria for measuring the performance of a school are difficult to determine without profitability, one of the benefits that would accrue to the for-profit school, several claimed, would be satisfactory educational accountability. Some discussion arose on the possibility of a deferred payment or pay-as-you-go plan, a good implementation, they maintained, of full-cost tuition.

There again recurred the question that persistently bothered at least two of the participants: Can we be sure that if the government does not support education, the private sector will? If there is no large demand for some desirable kind of school (for example, a school of classical studies), how will it be supported? Dependence wholly upon the market would reduce the university to the level of a trade school; it would destroy a culture, Dr. Kirk declared. But we cannot be sure what the market will offer, others insisted, who were convinced that someone will want to see a certain kind of school established and so will pay for it out of his taxed income. Admittedly, they said, government throughout history has subsidized a number of beautiful and worthy museums, galleries, libraries, and so on. Yet even so, they argued, that does not make it moral to force one man to pay taxes to support the scheme of another man whose object he may not favor. But the university is an exceptional case, Dr. Dietze once more asserted, for which he even was willing, if necessary, to relinquish his principle of liberalism in order to insure the long-range survival of the institution. If the private sector offered no university and the public authorities would guarantee independence for a state school, then Dr. Dietze would accept the state institution as better than no university at all. Other participants refused to consider that a state guarantee of independence could be anything more than mere words.

A spirited discussion on the practical solution of vouchers, or tuition chits, given by the state to students to use at the university of their choice, split the group in two. None wanted the voucher system as more than a makeshift, temporary arrangement, a halfway house, which moved some to comment on the scant likelihood of the state ever tearing down a halfway house. Dr. Roche stated that because government control always follows government money, if we object to government control of education we must veto this entering wedge. Private schools have never been a powerful element in this country, he went on. But the voucher system might be successful enough to invite controls, hence destroying the private schools already in existence. If one wants to win an argument in the long run, Dr. Roche stressed, he must stand absolutely and uncompromisingly on principle.

Be practical, admonished another participant; the breakdown of public education in the United States will not lead to private education but to Soviet model reforms or the kibbutz. If some halfway house is possible, then seize on it; do not reject it because it is not ideologically pure.

Every decision we make is a choice between imperfections, another participant refuted him. Which choice is the least imperfect or the most hopeful depends upon our ideal, upon where we want to go. The voucher plan would lead us down a path we do not want to follow.

Who will attend the university in the free society? The traditional plan of admitting those who pass entrance requirements and who can pay, either from their own funds or through scholarships, was one answer. Other participants seconded the position paper in advocating elimination of all entrance requirements save the ability to pay, either by oneself or through a voluntary donor. Such a plan, they hoped, would allow education for anyone who has the motivation to finance himself. It would not cater only to an intellectual or cultural elite.

The final issue of the discussion on mechanics of the university in a free society, touched upon only sporadically, was curriculum and method of educating. Participants ran the gamut from advocating elimination of nearly all electives to allowing students complete choice of courses. Several participants indicated the desirability of including in a liberal arts program a course in Anglo-American legal history—a substantive study of the historic cases themselves, not simply a survey on legal method.

Everyone espoused the system of lectures, tutorials and seminars—although some emphasized lectures more heavily than did the position paper. Finally, in a lively debate the participants argued the merits of objective versus essay examinations. One person refused to bow to attacks upon the objective test, calling it a good indicator of what students really know. Others defended the essay examination as a disciplinary exercise in critical thinking.

In summation, the participants concluded that a continuation of the public school system would only multiply the difficulties that plague our present structure. Though not altogether in harmony upon a precise definition of freedom or a free society, they did agree that a limited-government, free-market framework would provide the optimal conditions in which people might properly educate their children. Rather than public schools, then, they unanimously preferred private institutions. All but two participants rejected state control of education in any instance. State activity in the business of education, most participants agreed, even in education in the principles of a free society, is likely to lead to an insidious enslavement. Therefore, the state may neither subsidize nor compel education. Thus, making a choice among imperfections, the members of the Liberty Fund seminar chose to erect as their ideal educational system strictly private institutions operating in the framework of a state whose only interference would be to monopolize force for the protection of the rights of individual citizens.

Education
in a Free Society

Benjamin A. Rogge
Pierre F. Goodrich

Benjamin A. Rogge is Distinguished Professor of Political Economy, Wabash College (Crawfordsville, Indiana). He also serves as Director of the Wabash Institute for Personal Development, a summertime, liberal arts-based program in management development. In addition to his teaching, he has served as the Dean of the College at Wabash (1956–64); as a Visiting Lecturer, University of São Paulo (Brazil); as a lecturer in various executive programs on university campuses; and as a speaker to business and professional groups.

His articles on economics and education have appeared in various professional journals, and he is the co-author (with J. V. Van Sickle) of an introductory textbook in economics. He serves on the board of directors of various business and charitable organizations, including the Foundation for Economic Education and Liberty Fund, Inc.

Professor Rogge holds degrees from Hastings College (A.B., 1940), the University of Nebraska (M.S., 1946), and Northwestern University (Ph.D., 1953).

Pierre F. Goodrich is a graduate of Wabash College and the Harvard Law School. After a brief period of practicing law, he became involved in the public utility, mining, and banking business. For many years he was Chairman of the Board of Ayrshire Collieries Corporation (now a division of American Metal Climax, Inc.). He has been and is President of Indiana Telephone Corporation and of Peoples Loan & Trust Company of Winchester, Indiana. Mr. Goodrich has been deeply concerned with education and served as a trustee of Wabash College and the China Institute in America until recently. He is currently a Trustee of the Foundation for Economic Education, Inc., and a member of the Mont Pelerin Society. He is the founder and Chairman of three educational foundations: the Winchester Foundation, Liberty Fund, Inc., and Thirty Five Twenty, Inc.

The question is this: What would be the ideal educational arrangements in human society and, in particular, in a society of free and responsible beings?

Some Explanations and Assumptions

First of all, the presence in the question of the word "human" immediately takes from the word "ideal" any sense of the utopian. The question that we are asking is not how to produce Philosopher Kings or Ubermenschen, but, rather, how to do the best that is possible with the imperfect material that man now (and forever) represents. Our search is for a description of the optimal, not the perfect. Even the optimal in human affairs must, of necessity, reflect the underlying imperfection in the human raw material. But even this optimal set of arrangements is only a guideline, a Polaris to be used as a reference point by the navigator and not a position likely to be reached in fact.

Why then bother with an attempt to define that which would be less than perfect even if attained, but which is thought probably unattainable as well? Because without a reference point, the navigator is condemned to aimless wandering in an almost limitless sea of choice. *The identifying of an ideal is a matter of absolute practical necessity in all rational decision-making.* Far from being the impractical, time-wasting pursuit of the dreamer, an attempt to define the ideal is the first step of the rational man concerned with the conduct of each day's practical affairs.

Second, what precisely is meant by the word "imperfect," as used above to describe the human condition? First, it is assumed that man is imperfect as an intellectual agent; i.e., in his knowledge of himself and of the human and physical world around him. Next, it is assumed that man is imperfect as a moral agent; i.e., that he is of less-than-perfect integrity in serving whatever guidelines of ethical conduct he may recognize, in serving whatever ultimate purposes he may select. Next, it is assumed that man is imperfect as a Divine agent; i.e., he does not fully know or understand *what* he is, *why* he is, or what his role is in the cosmic scheme of things. In a word, he is not God. As John Locke said, a man cannot be a judge in his own cause. Finally, we accept the Acton thesis that it is man's nature for these inherent imperfections to become even more pronounced as he exercises power over others, particularly the power to coerce.

To summarize, in defining man as imperfect, we are describing him as an ignorant, weak creature, somewhat lower than the angels, with a strong predisposition to be corrupted by power. None of this is written as a hymn of despair or as a criticism of man or as the preface to a sermon to man to mend his evil ways; it is written as a description of that which is and will be. Man is not now God, he cannot acquire Godship, his greatest corruption is his desire to play God. In all this he seems not to have changed since the time when we first have knowledge of his characteristics. It would seem safe to assume that it is this imperfect raw material out of which must come whatever results can be obtained in human affairs. Again, to say this is not to despair; those who have truly lost hope for man are those who abandon him as he is and will be and create dreamworlds peopled with creatures that never have been and never will be on the face of this earth.

Third, we shall describe as "educational" any process that results in growth in understanding for a particular human being. We direct your attention immediately to our conviction that "education" is something that happens within an individual. No matter how formally educational the setting or the process, if nothing happens to the supposed learner, nothing educational has taken place. (*It should be apparent from this definition that perhaps the greater part of the activity now undertaken by supposed teachers and supposed students is not, in fact, educational at all.*) At the same time, something educational can take place far removed from a classroom, a teacher, a degree-granting institution, or any of the other paraphernalia of organized schooling. It would be difficult to over-estimate the importance we attach to the ideas that we have introduced in this paragraph (and which we will develop at greater length in a later section of the paper).

Fourth, given the almost infinite variability of the members of the human race, it seems safe to assume that we differ, one from the other, in our capacities to become educated, to acquire understanding in the various areas of knowledge. One will be more generally educable than another, one will be highly responsive in one area but not in another, one will respond to an educational technique to which another is unresponsive, etc. . . . It would seem to follow that no *one* approach to education would be optimal for all. Rather, the ideal set of educational arrangements we are seeking to describe must somehow take into account the fact of human differentiation.

Finally, the "educated man," as we have implicitly defined him here, is not necessarily also the "virtuous man," the "good man," the "great man," or the saint. We are not certain precisely how man does become virtuous or good or great or saintlike (perhaps through "revealed" knowledge?), but we are certain that it is not the necessary end product of education, not even of the ideal education that we hope to describe here. We are reluctant to believe that a man can be truly good, yet essentially ignorant (witness the many economic and political catastrophes wished on us by the apparently well intentioned but uninformed), but we do suspect that the saint and the scholar are not necessarily one and the same.

It might be possible to argue that the extensive knowledge of consequences of human actions which would come from being truly educated would lead a man to choose virtuous behavior, if on no other grounds than that of efficiency; i.e., the knowledge that right action succeeds while wrong action fails. But the Faust myth still rises to challenge us, and we cannot be comfortable with the assumption that the knowledgeable man will also be the noble or virtuous man. In fact, in the Faust myth, it is precisely the most learned who is most susceptible to the temptations of the Devil, to the lure of temporal power over others. (It is tempting to explain the behavior of many modern intellectuals in somewhat this way.)

We are aware, then, of the limitations of even the ideal that we hope to describe; even the best of all possible educational arrangements cannot make man into God or into a saint—or even into a good, decent human being. To be educated in the sense we have in mind here is something, perhaps a very important something, but it is not the alpha and the omega of human existence.

From these words of introduction, we turn now to our task. We shall ask, first, what are the purposes to be served by the educational arrangements we have in mind; then, what economic and political arrangements for education would seem best to serve those purposes; finally, what kinds of specific educational techniques we would expect to be emphasized in the ideal arrangements we seek to describe.

The Purposes of Education

A Preliminary Statement

Our concern is with, and only with, the purposes of education in a society of free and responsible men. Quite obviously, the purposes of education in an *un*free society are going to be directed to the needs of the ruler or the ruling group, whether it be a personal dictator, the dictatorship of the proletariat, the rule of the priest-kings, or what have you.

Some interesting technical questions are posed by the role and nature of education in unfree societies—questions that shed some light on the role of education in a free society. For example: Would it be in the interests of the rulers really to encourage (or even permit) growth in understanding among the ruled?

Or would all so-called education be, in fact, nothing more than training for the particular roles to be filled in the command-determined structure of society? Can all growth in understanding really be prevented, even by an apparently omnipotent state? Some of the great masterpieces of the human spirit that have been composed within prison walls would seem to testify to the durability of the desire for understanding and wisdom, at least on the part of the few. Further, there are questions of whether a dictatorship that really succeeded in stifling all true learning would not inevitably come to be staffed by men of such brittleness and inflexibility as to fall easy victim to some more imaginative foe.

Interesting though these questions may be, they are not our concern here. Here we seek to know only what would be appropriate in a free society. *By a free society, we mean precisely one in which each individual is free to do that which is peaceful;* or, put another way, one in which the state is limited to the role of the night watchman.

Put still another way, the properly educated citizens of a free society are those who are committed to living as responsible members of society, free from intimidation both by individuals within the society and by other nation states as well. (The question of how such a society should deal with those in its midst who are unwilling or unable so to live deserves serious attention, but will not be dealt with here. Briefly, it might be said that the hoped-for solution would lie in the growth in self-responsibility that often seems to follow upon the *necessity* of being responsible for self. The junior author of this paper is somewhat more optimistic about this coming about than is his partner.)

In such a society, the purpose to be served by any peaceful activity, whether it be educational, economic, religious, or what have you, is not a proper concern of the state; definitions of purpose lie wholly within the jurisdiction of the individuals involved. For example, whether the individual pursues an education for the sheer delight in learning or to acquire knowledge for personal decision-making and action or to better serve his God—or even to do no more than flaunt his learning before others—the choice of purpose (as well as means) is *his* and not society's.

In this sense, it is not only unnecessary to define the purposes of education in a free society, it is logically inconsistent to attempt to do so. The very meaning of the free society is a society in which questions of goals, ends, and purposes are left to the individual, and questions of means are of concern to the state only if the means used depart from the peaceful.

It would seem to follow from this that all that need be said about the educational arrangements in a free society is that they should be left to the free decisions of the individuals in the society, that the state should not interfere with any man's attempt to find the educational arrangements best suited to his purposes or with any man's attempt to offer educational arrangements that he thinks others might find attractive.

The Apparent Paradox

Comes now the seeming paradox. If, in a society already free, the state takes no action with regard to education, how can there be any assurance that the citizenry will know and understand the desirability of freedom, the various legal and other necessary structures of the free society, the undesirability of the unfree society? How will a citizenry not deliberately educated in the ways of freedom be able to withstand the constant temptations and pressures to abandon freedom in the hope of some transient advantage? In other words, does the survival of the free society require that its citizens be unfree in at least one area, the area of education? Must they be compelled to acquire at least some minimum of understanding of the nature of the free society, and its alternatives? Must all discussion of the alternatives to freedom be critical in nature, or can freedom be expected to win out in any open argument? Can even the free society afford to let educational arrangements be determined at the whim and caprice of its imperfect citizens?

Most self-styled free societies have chosen to abandon freedom in some degree in the field of education. Most have enacted compulsory school attendance laws;

most have used the coercive power of the state to obtain the funds to support some part or all of the formal educational programs in the society; most have dictated in one way or another, in one degree or another, what is and what is not to be taught in their schools and colleges.

A central argument of this paper is that *all* such interventions by the state in the educational process are both unnecessary and undesirable. We intend to argue that the best way for the people of a free society to assure that the educational arrangements of the society serve the cause of freedom is for the society *as a political unit* to have nothing whatsoever to do with those arrangements—except, of course, as the state protects the citizen from force and fraud in this area, as in all others.

We oppose state operation of educational programs at any level; we oppose state financing of such programs at any level, in any form (including tax relief); we oppose state coercion of participation in such programs, whether public or private. We believe that education must, by its nature, be a part of the *private* sector of society. We can hardly put our position more plainly or more forcefully.

But if the state (i.e., the night watchman) is not to educate for freedom, what persons or what agencies will? We remind the reader of two facts: (1) In even the largely free societies, the most effective spokesmen for limited government and individual freedom have usually *not* been the paid agents of the state. We offer the great historical examples of John Locke and, later, the authors of the *Federalist Papers*. (2) To grant to the government of even a free society authority over education, even for the intended purpose of educating for freedom, is to extend the power of fallible, corruptible men. And history reveals all too clearly how these men may yield readily to the temptation to turn education to the purposes of expanding state power (and, hence, their own power), rather than of restricting and limiting that power. Witness the many "civics" or "government" courses in modern America that are training grounds not for the defense of freedom but for attacks on freedom and limited government, in the interests of whatever social causes may be of current interest to the instructors.

We repeat: The task of educating individuals for freedom, if done at all, will be best done by *private* agencies and institutions, manned by individuals deeply committed to that cause. Admittedly, in a free society there will also exist private educational programs dedicated to restricting or eliminating freedom, alike manned by deeply committed individuals. Without being so naive as to believe that the truth must always win in an open contest, we still insist that the risk in this arrangement is far less than the risk run in a system where the agency of coercion (the state) is expected to educate the citizenry in the desirability of limiting the power of the state—a most unlikely act of self-denial!

In the words of one student of these questions, ". . . every politically controlled educational system will inculcate the doctrine of state supremacy sooner or later, whether as the divine right of kings, or the 'will of the people' in 'democracy.' "[1]

Whose Purposes, the Child's or the Parents'?

We have now made clear our insistence that the purposes of education are not to be defined by the state; they are rather to be defined by the individuals who participate in educational activities. This seems clear-cut enough in cases where the individuals involved are adults, assumed to be capable of making their own decisions. Certain questions arise when the participants are children.

Quite obviously, the infant is incapable of choosing a good part of what and how it is to learn, to grow in understanding of itself and of the world around it. But as the infant becomes the child and the child the young person and the young person the young adult, he (or she) tends to develop not only the capacity to make his own decisions but an ever-stronger will to do so as well.

Who should be entrusted with the decision-making

---

[1] Isabel Paterson, *The God of the Machine* (1943), pp. 271–72.

on educational questions for the infant and the child? —the parents or the legal guardians?—voluntary agencies concerned with child welfare?—the state? Who should decide when and to what extent the developing young person is to be permitted his or her own decision-making on educational matters?

There is a strong presumption among those who would use the state to bring about the good society to distrust the decision-making of the family in many areas, particularly in the rearing and educating of the young. In almost all of the better-known utopian schemes (e.g., those of Plato, Fourier, Robert Owen, and Skinner), the children are to be taken from their parents at an early age so that their upbringing can be under the control of the all-wise agents of the state, rather than of the foolish and primitive family circle.

Needless to say, while recognizing the serious, and at times tragic, imperfections of the family system of child raising, we reject all arrangements that would substitute for the imperfect family the even less perfect state. It is appropriate for the state to intervene in the family relationship when improper force is used against the child, and it may be necessary at times for the court to resolve questions of legal guardianships for orphan children. But except for those obvious cases, the state has no jurisdiction over the relationship of parent and child, including all questions of the education of the child.

The question of how much freedom of decision-making is to be granted the child by the parent is also a question for the parent to answer—not the state. Some parents will grant their children early and substantial freedom of decision-making on educational matters; others will insist on making all such decisions, even for offspring beyond the legal age dividing the child from the adult. Either attitude on the part of parents can be carried to absurd extremes, but it ill behooves us to ask the state to intervene in such cases, in view of the strong presumption we hold against state intervention in the peaceful activities of its citizens.

We repeat: Imperfect as it may be, the family still seems to be the *least* imperfect agency for the making of educational decisions for the young.

The ideal is that any given decision is to be made by the person or persons responsible for the consequences of the decision. In the case of education, this would seem to require that the parents (or guardians), for so long as they are financially responsible for the children, be permitted the associated right of making educational decisions for them. The child who becomes financially responsible for himself is no longer a child in this sense and should then be free to make his or her own educational plans.

Summary of the Purposes of Education

We have insisted that the very essence of a free society is that questions of purpose are to be resolved by the individuals involved. The purposes of education, then, must be personal and individual, to be chosen by the person directly involved or by those legally responsible for that person.

Even those of us who are deeply committed to the ideal of a society of free and responsible men and who would wish to see this ideal become a part of the understanding of all are restrained, by both principle and knowledge of consequences, from asking the state to make this ideal a part of the education of all. Our hope must rest in the uncertain outcome of competitive educational programs, free of state control. In a later section, we shall speculate on the nature of the noncoercive educational program that would seem to be most likely to develop in its participants an understanding of the free society and a commitment to it.

The Economics of Education

Some part of the education of each human being comes as the unintended by-product of the daily experiences of life. (See, for example, *The Education of Henry Adams.*) Education so gained may be painfully acquired, but in an economic sense, it is costless; i.e., no resources were taken from other possible uses to make this result possible. The opportunity cost of education so acquired is zero.

But the greater part of the education of a human

being requires the use of resources (if only the time of the person seeking the education) that could have been put to other uses. The questions that arise out of this fact are the ones now under study.

Types of Educational Activities and Institutions in a Truly Free Society

We begin by assuming a society in which the state plays no part in the educational process. Gone would be all state colleges and universities, all public elementary and secondary schools, all public libraries and public opera houses, and so forth. What would we expect to find in their places (if anything)?

Let us be honest. We do not know nor can we ever know, except by trying the experiment. As F. A. Hayek has demonstrated, it is impossible to predict the precise nature, the details, of what men will create under freedom.[2] Nor can we predict solely by studying the private sector of education under current arrangements. Under those arrangements, structure and performance of the private sector of education are distorted by a host of state interventions, including the awesome competition of a public rival who can give away that for which the private sector must ask a price.

We are not totally at a loss, though. We have been

---

[2] F. A. Hayek, "The Use of Knowledge in Society," *American Economics Review,* Vol. 35 (1945), pp. 519–30.

able to observe the private sector at work under relatively free circumstances in other lines of activity, and we can make some very rough guesses about the general nature of the educational arrangements under freedom.

First, we would expect enormous variety in the kinds, the forms, and the qualities of educational opportunities offered. For example, we would expect to see far more use than at present made of the relatively less expensive techniques of education—books, journals, tapes, films, televised lectures and discussions, and so forth. It has been in the interest of the educational establishment in this country to promote the demand for its own services (particularly the classroom teacher and the formal textbook) by emphasizing formal schooling over the almost infinite variety of less formal approaches to education. They may teach the children the story of the self-education of such greats as Abraham Lincoln or Thomas Edison, but only to emphasize the great disadvantage those men had to overcome in being denied the opportunities of the modern classroom, complete with its teacher with at least two degrees and 30 or more hours of course work in how-to-teach (but, perhaps, no true education). ("Just think what Lincoln could have accomplished had he been able to go to college!" was the statement of one such enthusiast to the senior author of this paper.) Capitalist enterprise has so reduced the cost of reading material that only the most desperately insolvent need now be denied at least this form of educational experience.

Next, we would expect many of the educational enterprises to be run for profit, hence to be more efficiently run than the not-for-profit enterprises that now control the greater part of education. (It is interesting to note the experiments now being conducted by some school boards, which, in their search for an answer to the gross inefficiencies of pubilc education, are turning to private, profit-making educational organizations to run their schools on performance-guaranteed contracts!) More on this later.

We would expect the formal schools in a free society to reflect at least as much variety as we now see in the private sector. Some would be operated by religious groups, some would be aggressively secular; some would be specialists in serving the gifted student, some in serving the slower students; some would have a variegated student body, some a homogeneous student body; some would offer only the liberal arts, others only the vocationally oriented materials, still others some mixture of the two. Actually, we would expect even more variety than that which now characterizes education; the current arrangements (as will be discussed later) do not lead schools to be consumer-oriented; the private school of the free society we have in mind would tend to reflect that same consumer-orientation that has characterized the private sector in other areas.

The Financing of Education

A convenient way to examine the issues under study here is to ask how education should be priced and whose funds should be used in paying that price.

The traditional view, even in largely free societies, is that education is somehow different from other goods and services and that this difference calls for special pricing and funding arrangements.

The differences are usually said to derive from two particular attributes of education: (1) the spillover of benefits from the individual to all of society, coming from the advantage of a better-educated citizenry; and (2) the unique importance of education to career opportunity and, hence, to providing some kind of equal opportunity for all.

These two claims have been discussed elsewhere by one of the authors of this paper.[3] To summarize the objections we have to these claims to special treatment of education: First, both the fact and degree of spillover benefits from education are open to serious question. In effect, what happens here is that A decides that C has been benefited by the education of B and that, therefore, C should pay some part or all of the costs of B's education. This is a denial of C's basic right to make his own decisions (in this as in other cases) about benefits supposedly flowing to him and to

---

[3] B. A. Rogge, "The Financing of Higher Education in the United States," *Wall Street Journal* editorial page, May 1, 4, 1959.

act accordingly. As a matter of fact, as two of the C's in modern America, we deny that we have gained from the schooling provided the B's; in fact, inasmuch as most of that schooling, as it relates to citizenship, has been antifreedom, we believe that we have been *damaged* by the schooling of the B's. For the state to tax us to support the teaching of collectivist ideas is a real violation of our freedom.

If the C's of this world believe that they would benefit by the B's understanding a specific educational activity, they are free to transfer resources directly or indirectly to the B's for that purpose. As a matter of fact, many of the schools and colleges of this country were founded by the C's on exactly this basis.

To the argument that the C's must pay for the education of the B's because, otherwise, the B's would not have an equal chance in the race of life, we reply: Given the infinite variability of the species, there is no way in which all individuals can start as equals, let alone end up as equals. To seek to provide so-called equality of opportunity would literally require the application of constant coercion to the human condition. *The only equality that is consistent with freedom is equality before the law;* in fact, this form of equality is a necessary condition for freedom to exist. All other forms and types of equalities can be brought into being (if at all) only through the use of force.

To put this another way: It is often said that each B has a *right* to an education. If a right exists, it must run against someone else, that is, against the C's of this world. This implies that each B that is brought into this world brings with him a blank check drawn on some collection of C's, to be cashed for whatever purposes society may decide appropriate. This is a monstrous perversion of the concept of natural rights —at least of the traditional interpretation of the natural rights idea.

Under the natural right concept as it flowered in the seventeenth, eighteenth, and nineteenth centuries, A, B, and C do indeed have certain rights with which they were endowed by their Creator, but those rights do *not* include rights to the goods and properties of each other. In fact, to John Locke, the right to one's own property is one of the natural rights; for another to claim that property as a right (to further his schooling, say) would be a denial of the *true* natural rights of man.

What B does have a right to, in the field of education, is to seek his education (or not seek it) by any peaceful means, free of the restraint and coercion of his fellow men. Not too surprisingly, this particular right is denied him daily by precisely those same A's who would award him an automatic claim on the goods and services of C for the purposes of education. (For example, in many states, the parents of a child are not permitted to provide schooling for that child in their own home, with themselves as the teachers.)

The concept that all must be assured of some form

of education, regardless of desire or financial ability, is thus rejected in principle. We would also question the practical argument that schooling is necessary to opportunity. We would argue that much of the apparent relationship between schooling and income either does not establish causation or reflects state action that has required degrees and diplomas as cards of admission to various careers.

Below-Cost Pricing and Efficiency

An additional pragmatic argument against providing "free" education to all is that this method of pricing produces gross inefficiencies in the educational process. (This argument is developed at length in the Rogge article previously cited.) First, under the system of tax-derived financing of schools, there is no natural process by which the efficiently run schools may grow and prosper and the poorly run schools be weeded out by the competition. One of the great achievements of the market process is that it does not suffer fools gladly, that it rather quickly takes the control of resources from the hands of the incompetent. One need not be a serious student of public education to be aware of the fact that a substantial part of the educational resources of this country are in the hands of the incompetent—yet this is inevitable under the current arrangements.

Next, this method of pricing does nothing to weed

out those students who have no desire to learn. The storekeepers (teachers, counselors, deans, etc.) must keep constant watch to see that the would-be customers do not slip out of the store without the merchandise that someone else has purchased for them—an absurd predicament. Admittedly, the young, under any system, are sometimes less than anxious to submit themselves to the discipline of education, but the problem is made much more severe (particularly at the secondary school level) by the fact that those who are anxious to learn are surrounded by the many who are not. Willingness to pay the price is one measure of strength of motive; when the price is zero, the motivation is often its equal.

In addition, with the income of the teacher coming *not* from the student but from a general subsidy, the teacher is under no real necessity of serving the interests of his students. One obvious manifestation of this is that in most public schools in this country, excellence (or lack of it) in teaching has absolutely nothing to do with the salary of the teacher. As Adam Smith put it:

> In other universities the teacher is prohibited from receiving any honorary or fee from his pupils, and his salary constitutes the whole of the revenue which he derives from his office. His interest is, in this case, set as directly in opposition to his duty as it is possible to set it. It is the interest of every man to live as much at his ease as he can; and if his emoluments are to be precisely the same, whether he does, or does not perform some very laborious duty, it

is certainly his interest, at least, as interest is vulgarly understood, either to neglect it altogether, or if he is subject to some authority which will not suffer him to do this, to perform it in as careless and slovenly a manner as that authority will permit. . . . In the University of Oxford, the greater part of the public professors have, for these many years, given up altogether even the pretense of teaching.[4]

In summary, then, *tax-supported education tends to make of our schools and colleges a collection of nonstudents under the tutelage of nonteachers and the administration of the incompetent.*

Summary of the Economics of Education

We reject, then, the view that education must be treated as a special case and insist, rather, that it be given precisely the same status as any other good or service in the marketplace. Let each man choose among the alternatives open to him; let each would-be supplier offer his wares in the marketplace, subject only to the general rules against fraud.

Note: In all probability, thanks both to the workings of the market and to the explicit application of the law against fraud, those conducting such educational programs would be brought to a higher level of integrity and honesty than now characterizes such men and institutions. The arrangements currently existing

---

[4] Adam Smith, *The Wealth of Nations* (Modern Library, n.d.), pp. 717–18.

in both public and private schools and colleges tend to induce administrators to deceive the students, the parents, the governing boards, the taxpayers, and/or the donors to their institutions as to the true nature of the school's operations. In particular, most college administrations have found it desirable, shall we say, *not to emphasize* the fact that on their campuses the students will be confronted by faculties far more liberal or left-wing than the *prevailing point of view* among parents, trustees, taxpayers, and donors. In how many college catalogs do you find prospective students and their parents given *any* information on the social philosophies to which the student is exposed on that campus? Do they say, "Send your son to College X and he will be taught by 5 Marxist, burn-down-the-buildings activists, 15 non-Marxist, just-seize-the-buildings activists, 100 left-of-center modern liberals, 10 Ripon Society Republicans, and 2 eccentric conservatives just reaching retirement age"? As Professor George Stigler of the University of Chicago has said, " . . . the typical university catalogue would never stop Diogenes in his search for an honest man."[5]

Quite obviously, there are dishonest men and men of questionable integrity in all occupations, but both competition and the law tend to weed them out over

---

[5] George Stigler, "The Intellectual and the Market Place," *Selected Paper*, No. 3, Graduate School of Business, University of Chicago, February 1967, p. 7.

a period of time in the market sectors of the economy. However, no such process works as vigorously in the not-for-profit sectors. A thoroughly dishonest man can probably last longer under the umbrella of occupational blessedness in teaching or the ministry than in the world of business.

To continue with the summary of the economics of education in a truly free society: Again, we cannot predict with accuracy the pattern that truly free men would develop to serve their educational desires. In general, though, we would expect a mixture of for-profit and not-for-profit institutions to prevail, with the for-profit institutions largely setting the pace, at least in terms of the economics of the operation. For example, we would expect that education would come to be priced in a market fashion, that is, with the equilibrium price being one that covers all costs, including a normal rate of return to ownership. Even the not-for-profit institutions would probably find it efficient and equitable to set prices at market levels, with subsidies going to individual recipients rather than to institutions. Few who wish to give bread to the poor think it wise to do this by starting a bakery and selling the bread to all (or even just to the poor) at below cost. Most find it more efficient to subsidize the individual (but not by the state) and then let him buy his bread where he will—and so we would expect it to be in the system we are describing here.

We would also expect school and college administrators to demand that teachers *really* serve the interests of students. We do not mean by this that the students would run the place but only that, as the ultimate consumers of the product, their decisions to stay or leave would determine whether the institution itself would survive. The faculty members who today can consistently shirk their teaching responsibilities just wouldn't be tolerated under the arrangements we have in mind—unless, of course, they could find some private source of funds to support them in whatever it is they are doing (such as research) other than teaching. (*Note:* Research and teaching are not necessarily mutually exclusive activities; in fact, the teacher who is not actively engaged in a continuing search for more understanding is not likely to be an effective teacher. We would expect some part of the financial reward for research to come in the form of the higher fees that students would pay to study with such teachers.)

The income of teachers, then, would be determined by the effectiveness with which they served the purposes of the employing institutions—not by seniority or degrees earned. Needless to say, the tenure arrangement would disappear. Both of the authors have discussed this topic in other writings.[6] Suffice it to say here that tenure is not needed by the competent and, hence, shields only the incompetent. We are not dis-

---

[6] B. A. Rogge, *op. cit.;* Pierre F. Goodrich, *Education Memorandum —1951–1969.*

suaded from this position by any arguments with reference to so-called academic freedom. *We simply do not
believe in academic freedom.* We do believe in the idea
that each man should be free to say what he will; but
we don't believe that any one has the right to say what
he will and be paid for the saying of it by someone else
who doesn't wish to so pay him! In this sense, academic
freedom is, in fact, a denial of freedom—the freedom
of each man to expend his resources on only those uses
that he sees fit—including the choice of sources of
learning.

We have no way of knowing how the advantages and
disadvantages of horizontal and vertical integration
would serve to shape the nature and form of educational institutions. Perhaps chain-store and full-line
education would emerge as the most efficient; perhaps
the independent or the specialty shop would prove the
more flexible and innovative. We simply don't know—
but we do know that whatever would emerge could not
help but be many times more efficient than the present
arrangements.

We must summarize by saying that *a truly private
educational system, rather than being more "costly"
than a public one, would surely provide more and
better educational opportunities at a far lower cost per
unit of delivered product (i.e., per unit growth in
knowledge) than the current system.*

We repeat: let each family, using its own resources
or resources voluntarily made available to it by others,

pay for such educational programs for its children as it sees fit—whether that which is purchased be a book, a television set, or four years at Harvard College. Let each adult, again using funds acquired by peaceful exchange or gift, make his or her own educational decisions, acting on them in the educational market-place. If freedom of choice is desirable for individuals in most aspects of their lives, why is it not imperative that freedom of choice be granted them in one of the most important aspects of their lives: their growth in understanding of themselves and of the world around them? To the collectivists we say, if you insist on controlling something, make it the peanut-butter or hula-hoop industries, but for God's sake, leave education alone!

The Ideal College

In this section, we intend to describe in some detail what we believe would be an ideal college. Let us say a number of things immediately:

1. These are no more than our own thoughts on what we would consider the ideal college. In a free educational marketplace, consumers might or might not select *our* ideal as *their* ideal—and their choices would be the ones that would prevail.

2. The criterion of "ideal" we are using is this: Does this arrangement maximize the likelihood that those who are exposed to it will come to be committed to the free society and, equally important, come to know and understand precisely what they are for and against and why? In other words, we are not interested in the purely emotional, unreasoning convert to our point of view.

Some might wish to argue that what we are proposing is a propaganda mechanism, not an educational program. To this we would make two replies: First, in the sense that there are no truly "objective" teachers or collections of teachers, all educational institutions have some kind of planned or unplanned slant or point of view. For example, most of the so-called places of "true learning" in this country today are, in fact, dominated by the philosophies of the left and, hence, giant factories of left-wing thought and opinion. Our position would be openly declared, for all to know, rather than concealed under the guise of objectivity. Second, it is our conviction that any person of reasonable intelligence who studies the human experience in the manner appropriate to true learning will probably come to the conclusion that the optimal organization of society is that of free and responsible men under limited government and the rule of law. Admittedly, some may not agree; certainty is rarely encountered in human affairs. Others may agree in principle but find the attractions of power for themselves too great to resist. (Compare, for example, the Woodrow Wilson who said, "The history of human liberty is the history of limitation of governmental power," with the Woodrow Wilson in the Presidency, who added enormously to the power of government in the domestic economy and who used his position to bring America's entry into a tragic foreign war. The poet Kipling reflected some rare insight in his poem "The Gods of the Copybook Headings," published in 1919.) In other words, we believe that true growth in understanding is likely to turn the learner's head and heart in the direction of freedom; the educational dice do not have to be loaded in our favor—although it may be necessary that they not be loaded against us, as they now are.

3. We have chosen the college-level kind of institution, not because it is necessarily the most important, but because we feel that we have had more experience with and know more about this kind of education than we do about, say, elementary schooling.

We would add only that we believe the same general principles would apply at all levels of true educational activity. In a truly free, competitive educational system, we would expect a great variety of elementary and secondary educational programs to evolve, some involving the formal classroom, others not. What we *would* expect to happen is that the young and the very young would come to some level of competence in the basic skills of language and number use at an earlier age and at far less expense per pupil than under current arrangements.

> 4. We are restricting our model to what might be termed (in a very rough sort of way) the liberal arts college.

We are not contemptuous of vocational training nor do we deny that much vocational training can also lead to true growth in general understanding in the liberal arts sense. However, the training of doctors or electrical engineers or lawyers need not have any close relationship to the question of freedom. Our concern is with those forms of educational activity that do seem to have a close tie to questions of human freedom. (Actually, we are convinced that the training of doctors, accountants, lawyers, engineers, or what have you, would be improved if greater general understanding were required of them. When the accountant, for example, encounters problems of inflation or of political control of his work, he stands in need, *even to be a better accountant,* of kinds of understanding not usually taught in courses in accounting.)

The Structure of the College

The college would be private, of course, with ownership and, hence, control residing in a specified person or group of persons. *Note:* Many of the problems of today's colleges and universities flow from the ambiguous nature of ownership and, hence, control. With students, faculty members, alumni, administrators, board members, taxpayers, donors, and the general public all laying claim to some authority, it is no wonder that it is sometimes difficult to determine who really is in charge.

The firm could be for-profit or not-for-profit, with our preference being for the former.

All decisions of policy would be made by the board and implemented by the administration. As in any successful firm, customer (student) and employee (faculty) opinion and responses would be made a part of the general information on which policymaking decisions would be based, but in no case would any ambiguity about the location of final authority be permitted.

Personnel Policies and Practices

Faculty members would be selected for their promise as teachers, in the sense of encouraging and contributing to growth in understanding in others.

The greater part of them (perhaps all) would be men and women who are also deeply committed to the philosophy of the free society: If we believe (as we do) that the outcome of true learning is likely to be such a commitment, then it would be inconsistent of us to seek to find true scholars and teachers among those not so committed. However, in recognition of our own fallibility and of the responses of students to what seem to be loaded dice, it might not be inappropriate for the faculty to include some who are critics of the free society.

Faculty members would serve at the pleasure of the administration, with only such recognition of time in service as is usually appropriate in any organization.

The income of faculty members would be directly related to their effectiveness in serving the purposes of the college. In effect, if they failed to attract students to their lectures or their seminars, or if nothing educational seemed to happen to those who did so attend, the man would be fired, or his salary not increased, or what have you. (An alternative arrangement would be for the greater part of faculty income to be in the form of student fees paid directly to them, after students have paid the college proper a basic fee to cover overhead expenses.[7])

The Curriculum

The educational program of the college would consist of three basic elements: (a) individual study by students, (b) seminars on assigned readings, and (c) lectures delivered by members of the faculty (or visitors).

---

[7] John Fischer, "Preface to the Catalogue of Curmudgeon College," *Harper's,* June 1970, pp. 75–78.

Students could choose among the alternatives available to them, with only these provisos: (a) any student whose behavior in class or on campus created problems for others would be asked to leave; (b) any student who wished to participate in a given seminar would be expected to have read the assigned material. On evidence that he had not read the material, the seminar leaders would ask him to leave (or perhaps, become an observer only).

For any given term, the college would publish a list of the seminars to be held and of the lectures to be given. These lists would be the basis on which students could plan their programs. On such questions, students could consult counselors explicitly provided by the administration or any member of the faculty who would consent to serve. Students would also be given a list of suggested books and other materials, including not only those to be explicitly discussed in seminars but readings that would contribute to the general understanding of the student. Some of the books that might be listed (in either category) are given in the Liberty Fund Memorandum, Part VI.

Students could continue for as many terms as they wished, given proper behavior in the classroom and on campus. *No degrees would be given or diplomas awarded.* The college would exist to serve students truly seeking knowledge, not those seeking only a degree or other meaningless relics from the current system.

Neither courses nor teachers would be organized by departments or divisions. Quite naturally, some range of interests in the faculty would be deliberately sought, but the artificiality of departmental lines would be avoided. *Note:* The *fact* of departmentalization for administrative purposes is not the great evil; it is the *spirit* of intellectual departmentalization that we would seek to avoid.

The Educational Process

Students would involve themselves in reading, discussing, and listening to lectures—and we would put them in that order, both in terms of importance and of the chronological order in which they should take place. In effect, students would be sent off to do some guided reading, then brought together for small group discussions under trained Socratic leadership, then more reading and more discussion. Finally, the student would be ready to listen intelligently to lectures presented on the topics under study—then more discussion, more reading, and so forth.

Students who wished to receive an evaluation of their progress could make appropriate arrangements, including payment of fees recognizing the extra work involved in such an evaluation. They could write papers or examinations to be read by members of the faculty and used as the basis of evaluation. No grades in the usual sense of that term would be given, except at the request of the student or his parents (or some person or agency providing the student with financial assistance). We suggest this arrangement not because we are opposed to competition for excellence among students, but because the real purpose of education is for each individual to make the maximum progress possible *for that person*—for this, relative judgments are not significant.

The Student Body

The student body would be made up of those who would be attracted by this kind of educational program and who would be willing to pay the full cost of participating in it. Without the artificial lure of degrees, college dances, and campus sit-ins, we would expect an appropriate student body to be self-selecting.

In Loco Parentis?

The remarks made above should not be taken to mean that we object to young people going to dances or doing other things that they find enjoyable. We are not opposed to fun—we just don't believe that it is the business of the college to organize, sponsor, or finance it.

The college would not take responsibility for the general lives of its students; it would not serve *in loco parentis*. Some colleges might choose to do so (for a price), but not this one. Parents who might wish to see their sons or daughters under what they would think appropriate supervision could undoubtedly arrange with local families or landladies for this supervision to be given.

We give you then Free Society College, a sample of the kind of school that might emerge in a free educational marketplace. If this particular college is not to your liking, you need have no fear that it would be the only kind available. We would expect every conceivable type of formal and informal educational program to be available at a wide range of prices. One of the great advantages of the economic over the political marketplace is that the majority does *not* rule. Every minority opinion that can be served with any hope of profit can and will be served.

Summary

We have argued in this paper that the educational arrangements currently in use in this country are grossly inefficient, inequitable, contrary to human rights, contrary to human nature, and destructive of the society of free and responsible men. We have sought to construct a general picture of those arrangements in education that would be ideal, in terms of being consistent with the principles and practices of a free society and of tending to produce individuals knowledgeable about and committed to that free society. We have rejected any possibility that the ideal could involve state participation and have argued that the ideal arrangements must be found within the jurisdiction of the private educational marketplace. As an example of the kind of school that might emerge under freedom, we have sketched the general features of a college program that we believe would serve the cause of its students and of the free society.

It seems unlikely that the American society will move rapidly (if at all) in the directions we have indicated. But this we do know: if there are none in the society who stand ready to hold out the ideal of a more hopeful arrangement, real progress is not only unlikely—it is forever impossible.

Essay One

Reason of University

Gottfried Dietze

Gottfried Dietze graduated from the law school of the University of Heidelberg and received doctorates in philosophy from Princeton and in juridical science from the University of Virginia. A professor of political science at The Johns Hopkins University, he was a visiting professor at the University of Heidelberg and the Brookings Institution. He is the author of Uber Formulierung der Menschenrechte *(1956),* The Federalist *(1960),* In Defense of Property *(1963),* Magna Carta and Property *(1965),* America's Political Dilemma *(1968),* Youth, University and Democracy *(1970),* Bedeutungswandel der Menschenrechte *(1971),* Academic Truths and Frauds *(1972),* Two Concepts of the Rule of Law *(1973), and is now completing a book on rights and riots. Dr. Dietze has participated in a number of Liberty Fund's seminars.*

Reason of State

Until recently, few people would have thought of "reason of university" as a concept similar to "reason of state." While universities may have been dependent upon, and threatened by, popes, kings, popular majorities, and demagogues, no doctrine of reason of university developed. Much as unreasonable practices, false intrigues, cowardice, and intellectual sacrifices may have existed in institutions which supposedly were to serve the truth irrespective of personal sacrifices, they generally did not overshadow the traditional image of the university as a lighthouse for the exploration of the truth. As long as universities were considered bastions of reason, there seemed to be no reason to think of reason of university.

This has changed. Recent student unrest, which has threatened the very existence of universities, has brought into focus the question of what those ruling universities must do for the protection and preservation of institutions that can be considered vital for the progress of civilization. A discussion of reason of university has become imperative. Paraphrasing Meinecke's introductory sentences to his work on reason of state, we may well state: "REASON OF UNIVERSITY is the fundamental principle of academic conduct, the university's first Law of Motion. It tells the academic statesman what he must do to preserve the health and strength of the university. The university is an organic structure whose full power can only be maintained by allowing it in some way to continue growing; and *reason of university* indicates both the path and the goal for such a growth."[1]

At first sight, the idea of reason of university will give us pause. It reminds us of reason of state and frightens us. For reason of state demonstrates what is demoniac in power, "an innately human, perhaps even animal urge which blindly engulfs everything until it is halted by external forces."[2] Hitler and Stalin and other cruel dictators come to mind. So does the

---

[1] Friedrich Meinecke, *Machiavellism: The Doctrine of Raison d'Etat and Its Place in Modern History* (1957), p. 1.

[2] Friedrich Meinecke, *Strassburg-Freiburg-Berlin 1901–1919* (1949), p. 194. See Walther Hofer's introduction to Friedrich Meinecke, *Die Idee der Staatsräson in der neueren Geschichte* (1957), p. xxvi.

absolutism of the *ancien régime,* reflected in Louis XIV's statement, *L'Etat c'est moi.* We are reminded of the *arcana imperii,* the Star Chamber, the Inquisition, of cruel punishments that were not unusual in the so-called Age of Reason, an age marred by the practice of reason of state. We see ruthless exploitation by those wielding power not merely of the principle that the end justifies the means but of the idea that any end, even the most oppressive and unethical state, justifies any means for its own preservation.

Frightening as the thought of reason of state may be, our fear is likely to decrease as we take a closer look at it. It is obvious that the employment of dubious means for ethical ends is more defensible than the use of such means for immoral ends. And it is assuring that even Machiavelli, generally considered the originator of the doctrine of *ragione di stato,* is perhaps offering less encouragement to "Machiavellians" than they would like. The question has been asked whether the problems connected with reason of state really arise in the Florentine's writing because this concept derived from his considering the state a prerequisite for *virtù,* an idea current at his time, hard to translate and never defined by him. While some authors have maintained that Machiavelli's conception of *virtù* connotes the qualities of a successful highway robber,[3]

---

[3] Jacques Maritain, *La Fin du Machiavellisme* (1941); G. Toffanin, *Machiavelli e il Tacitismo* (1921); and *Il Cinquecento* (1929).

others have likened it to the Greek *arete* and the Roman *virtus*. They considered *virtù* the congeries of qualities required of the citizen of a constitutional republic such as Athens or Rome, implying manliness not only in the sense of courage and prowess but also in the sense of self-discipline and steadfastness; a willingness to fight but also a willingness to sacrifice oneself for the *patria;* a determination to succeed but also a recognition of the civic obligation to serve.[4]

Still, even in case of the latter interpretation the various ethical aspects of *virtù* suggest values that are debatable. It is questionable whether manliness in the form of courage and prowess is better than in the form of self-discipline or steadfastness, whether a determination to succeed is preferable to a recognition of civic obligations, and whether any of these values justifies arbitrary and cruel measures for reason of state. The same applies to values mentioned by authoritarian followers of Machiavelli, be they Bodin's *salus populi,* Botero's well-being of the Church, or others.

The situation is not much different in the case of the defenders of "constitutional reason of state," men who have tried to protect political orders in which governmental power was limited for the sake of freedom. These men were classified into "survivalists" like Harrington, Spinoza, and Montesquieu; "Christians" like Calvin, the Calvinists, and Althusius; "moralists" like

---

[4] Carl J. Friedrich, *Constitutional Reason of State* (1957), p. 18.

Milton, Locke, and Kant; and, standing all by himself, Hegel, whom Meinecke had treated as an absolutist Machiavellian.[5] The variety of these authors suggests that their values are as diversified as those presented by the authoritarian proponents of reason of state. Again, this raises questions as to the priority of values, and whether any one of those values justifies governmental actions, even for constitutional reason of state, designed for the preservation of *Rechtsstaaten* that protect the rights of men and employ means which generally are less dubious than those permitted by the absolutists.

If there is any value worth preserving in a collective body, it is the freedom of the individual from the government, the value for the preservation of which men are believed to have freely entered societies and which is inherently restricted in collective bodies. Since constitutionalism has grown with that freedom, it probably reached its climax in the liberal state of the nineteenth century. Under that form of government, doubts concerning reason of state arise the least, and the doctrine of constitutional reason of state seems to be the most defensible. We may call it "liberal reason of state." As a matter of fact, it may be asked whether liberal reason of state can be considered reason of state, a concept with which we traditionally have connected oppressive government action for the sake of a more

---

[5] *Ibid.*

or less dubious state and its more or less dubious ideals. Still, this question must be answered in the affirmative. Believers in classic liberalism must never forget the basic rule of liberalism: the freer a society, the stricter must be the enforcement of its laws. The more liberal a state, the more imperative liberal reason of state.

Even freedom is a value about which one can disagree. The many changes in the meaning of freedom[6] prove that so far we do not know its true scope in civil society. Men have employed many devices to find out, dividing freedom, for example, into its component parts and establishing categories, such as freedom from the government and freedom to participate in government, and breaking up these categories into various liberties. But these methods have not yet succeeded in letting us know all about freedom. As a matter of fact, they have confronted us with new problems, concerning, for instance, the priorities of the various categories or liberties. These uncertainties make us question the value of liberties and freedom anew. We ask whether even liberal reason of state is justified.

In summary, we must entertain doubts about any type of reason of state. We should gravely fear the use of dubious means for dubious ends. Our fears are reduced with respect to the kind of reason of state that perhaps Machiavelli and certainly some of his more

---

[6] Gottfried Dietze, *Bedeutungswandel der Menschenrechte* (1971).

ethical followers had in mind, that is, permitting the use of dubious means for less dubious ends. Those fears are further reduced in the case of constitutional, and especially liberal, reason of state. Yet always, doubts remain.

Reason of University

We need have no doubts about reason of university. This concept, new as we introduce it, does not have the bad connotations of reason of state. It need not be feared. Fear of examinations and exmatriculations aside, universities are not institutions which can interfere with the rights of the individual unless the individual agrees to such an interference. *Volenti non fit iniuria* is a paramount principle of the university order. Universities have disciplinary power and can request fees. However, they cannot deprive anyone of his life, liberty, or property against his will.

If there need be no fear of reason of university on account of the absence of a compulsory university order, there also need be no apprehension concerning the university's aims. While doubts can be entertained about the values of states, such as religion, discipline, civic obedience, and even freedom, there can be no doubt about the paramount value of universities, namely, the truth. Truth is a value which is, by definition, beyond doubt. Its absolute validity is so indisputable that other values seem to become irrelevant. Truth may thus be said to be the teleological apex of "value-freeness" (in the sense of the proponent of the truth-seeking university, Max Weber[7]), thereby actually being the supreme of all values. Other values that are human can also be humane. Truth is humane by definition.

It is true that states also have their truths, and all too often they leave no doubts about them. But all too often are we aware that these truths are human but by no means humane. They are based on debatable values, ideologies, and *Weltanschauungen* which frequently have turned out to be mere half-truths, if not pure lies. Their values are mainly political. Whether or not one agrees with Schmitt's conception of the political as being a concept of friend and foe, implying the annihilation of the one by the other,[8] there is some truth to it. Political values are likely to conflict, even in liberal societies. *Wert* (value) is not just opposed to *Unwert* (nonvalue), the worthy to the "unworthy" life, class, race, or religion, as under authoritarian states. *Wert* is also opposed to *Gegenwert* (countervalue), as present discussions in pluralistic societies on social welfare, civil rights, and other issues attest. However, even in societies where there is less of an either/or attitude than is found in their authoritarian counterparts,

---

[7] Max Weber, *Wissenschaft als Beruf* (1919).

[8] Carl Schmitt, *Der Begriff des Politischen* (1932).

one value or set of values will usually dominate, oppose, and often condemn other values. Although, because of constitutional protections, such a condemnation will usually not result in annihilation, it often will bring about the mutilation or depowerization of values that are not "in."

It is also true that in universities men favoring certain ideas will oppose, and often condemn, the ideas of others. This is evident not only in value-prone disciplines, such as theology, the humanities, and the social sciences, but also in such disciplines as the natural sciences. Universities are places for constant evaluations and counterevaluations, the abodes not only of *Methodenstreit* but also of disputes on whether what has been found through research methods is the truth. Still, the values of scholars are different from those of citizens. Scholars "value" something merely because they think it reflects the truth. Citizens, on the other hand, value things such as peace and war, socialism and free enterprise, because they believe them to be opportune and perhaps virtuous.

The truth, basically, is a nonpolitical value and less disputable than political values. While it is opposed by the lie, the lie is as little dangerous to the truth as is nonsense to sense. It has no value and can thus constitute no countervalue comparable to the countervalues of political values. Also, countertruth can only be something that reveals that a so-far-accepted "truth" is false, and thus must be conducive to the truth itself.

As opposing countertruths to supposed truths has been the lifeblood of universities, university life has been characterized by a constant defense against political power. Just as *studium,* originally meant to complement *sacerdotium* and *imperium,* turned into a challenge of the latter two and, in turn, became challenged by them, universities as centers of study, orginally founded to support popes and kings, came to challenge them and were, in turn, challenged by them. The history of universities thus not only demonstrates how, for the sake of the truth, assumed truths were challenged by countertruths. It also shows how institutions committed to the truth were attacked by governments which tried to impose their political values, believed to be opportune and sometimes virtuous, upon the universities, for reason of state. The doctrine of reason of state has thus been barbarously used as a defense for what those in power felt to be virtues. To the degree to which these "virtues" were opposed to a free exploration of the truth, they can only be considered pseudovirtues.

This "barbarism of virtue"[9] has threatened universities also in modern democracies. Perhaps that threat is greater than it was during the age of absolutism. True, universities became freer as absolutism was superseded by constitutional government, a development to which

---

[9] Cf. Sidney Hook, "The Barbarism of Virtue," *PMLA,* 84 (1969), p. 465.

universities contributed their fair share. On the other hand, attacks upon universities became more diversified as the few values of monolithic absolutism were replaced by the many values of pluralistic societies. For instance, whereas formerly universities were attacked because they challenged values such as nationalism, militarism, the police state, and mercantilism, in pluralistic societies universities could come under fire for challenging not only the values just mentioned but also their countervalues, such as cosmopolitanism, antimilitarism, civil government, and free trade, as well as other values. In short, universities can now be attacked for not sharing any particular opinion that any particular group or individual might happen to hold.

Attacks upon universities probably have also become more intense. In spite of the greater diversity of threats, universities were better off under constitutional government than under the *ancien régime*. The pluralism inherent in liberal democracy made it likely that attacks on universities, based as they would be upon a great variety of values and reasons, would countervail each other. This would prevent the universities' being assaulted by one overwhelming power, which, like a wedge, would intrude into their lives and destroy them. However, the situation changed once limited democracy developed into sheer majority rule. Now universities could be attacked not only by those who happened to believe in different values and whose eagerness was likely to be intensified by the hope of powerfully representing the majority one day, but also by those who actually held power and whose attack would be quite formidable because it was backed by the unrestricted majority. Absolute as it has become, modern democracy thus contains a combination of the dangers that are inherent in both absolutism and liberalism. Therefore, universities must be on their guard not only against a multitude of attacks from minor groups but also against concerted attacks from the omnipotent majority. The universities' vulnerability seems to have grown since the ages of absolutism and constitutionalism or limited democracy. For during the former, universities only had to watch out for the concerted attack of the monarch, and during the latter, such attacks were improbable because of the countervailing forces of constitutional pluralism.

American universities have experienced both kinds of attacks. When pluralism was abundant, many colleges and universities were founded by local and sectional groups who had their specific religious, spiritual, political, etc., values. On the face of it, the orientation of these institutions toward these values seemed to be, and often was, incompatible with the paramount aim of the university, the pursuit of the truth. On the other hand, many of these institutions were founded and controlled not only with the view of promoting values dear to the founders but with a view of promoting the truth. For that reason, educational diversity thus established actually was conducive to the truth because different approaches inevitably aid in finding the truth. The chances for a successful pursuit of the truth were further enhanced by universities that were not committed to specific civic, religious, or political values.

The situation changed when, following the march of democracy that had been envisaged by de Tocqueville, there came about a national social ideology, which was bolstered by an aggressive majority and came to influence the values of universities throughout the nation. Aided by the decline of federalism and the separation of powers, institutions that had contributed to preventing a concentrated ideological challenge to universities, the New Deal ushered in a revolution that was as far-reaching in education as it was in the political and social spheres. Roosevelt's Brain Trust ended up as the universities' brain bust. From now on, more and more professors would consider themselves New and Fair Dealers, New Frontier and Great Society men, rather than scholars. Universities moved toward the left, a move which shocked the young Buckley at Yale but which was a nationwide phenomenon.[10] It is one of the great paradoxes that as academic freedom received greater recognition than ever before, it became more and more a monopoly of those who tended toward the left; McCarthyism seemed to have made the leftists

---

[10] William F. Buckley, *God and Man at Yale* (1951); Russell Kirk, *Academic Freedom* (1955).

immune to accusations that they were ideologists rather than scholars and that their values were political rather than academic.

The members of the present left can well afford to attack universities as bluntly and violently as they have. Sheltered by anti-McCarthyism and anti-anti-communism, accusations that they work for a foreign power or for the communists have helped rather than hurt them. While they officially have turned against the "establishment," they actually are outgrowths of an establishment that has consistently moved to the left. The fact that the activities of student radicals have found sympathy with faculty as well as administrative officials or have been, at best, opposed lukewarmly, shows how basically akin faculty and officials feel toward the aims of these radicals. Indeed, it must be difficult for faculty and administrators who are not free from New Deal or New Frontier ideology to effectively combat those who just go a little farther, who, in a way, are the children released by the ideological establishment in universities.

Our ideologists need not be surprised about the wrath of those children. Having taught them that property rights do not rank as highly as the "preferred freedoms" of democratic rights, that social legislation ought to absolve debtors and "underdogs" from their contractual obligations, the ideologists should not be shocked to see students refuse to honor their contractual obligations toward the universities by inter-

fering with the ordinary process of learning, and
to see them disregard property rights by occupying
buildings, setting them on fire, or bombing them.
Having all along considered it poor taste to criticize
communism and having even emphasized its virtues,
professors need not be surprised to see students raise
the clenched fist, wave red flags, and admire and use
the guerrilla tactics of Che Guevara and the Vietcong.
After universities degenerate from institutions serving
the truth to institutions serving the community and its
ever-changing values—not realizing that exploring the
truth is the greatest service to the community—it seems
only natural that students would want universities to
follow the ever-changing ideals of the student community (today more teaching and less research, to-
morrow a new calendar, the day after no ROTC, still
later no military recruiting on campus, more coeds,
pass-fail grades, no research for war purposes, and so
on and on and on and on), rather than to adhere to
the constant ideal of the free exploration of the truth.

I do not want here to sit in judgment on the values of
leftist administrators, faculty, and students. I think
quite a few of them are sincere in their beliefs. Peace,
the welfare of the people, democracy, freedom, and
equality are indeed values to be cherished. And although
my concepts of those values are in many respects quite
different from those of my leftist colleagues, I admit
that I have as little a monopoly on the truth as they do.
The more do I resent that they have acted as if they

had a monopoly on the truth and under the label of liberalism have tried to impose their values upon others through force and violence, in as illiberal a fashion as can be imagined. Rather than peacefully discussing them in the forum of truth, the universities, they have set out to destroy that forum. I do not at all deny their right to discuss their values in school. While Weber wanted politics kept out of the classroom, the open and rational discussion of political problems is as much part and parcel of academe as is the search for new data in the natural sciences. But the leftists have jeopardized such a discussion by turning universities into emotional theaters. Whereas many a truthful idea can result from an emotional outburst, this is an exception to the rule that most truthful ideas are revealed through reason. The exception ought not to become the rule. However much we may cherish our values, and no matter how virtuous we may consider them—and ourselves—those values ought not be permitted in an arrogant way to destroy universities and challenge the supreme virtue of truth.

Present threats to universities in modern democracies, then, jeopardizing as they do the free exploration of the truth in the manner of absolutist and totalitarian regimes which sacrificed the idea of the university for reason of state, call for an implementation of the doctrine of reason of university. That doctrine is far-reaching and includes the institutional organization of the university as well as university policy.

From what has been said, it follows that universities cannot be rubberstamps of societies and their governments, including democracy. Whereas in most societies there is goodwill toward an exploration of the truth, that will is generally frustrated by the desire for convenience and the white lies and lies that go with it. Furthermore, goodwill alone probably cannot be a substitute for the ability necessary for the exploration of the truth. Quantity seldom will replace quality. Societies can have many excellent features, and democracies can be excellent forms of government. Still, the per capita excellence of societies will generally be below that of their universities. And only excellent individuals and institutions with a high per capita quality, such as universities, will be able to push toward the outer frontiers of knowledge. The statement that at a certain point of development the death of about a dozen leading physicists would have delayed nuclear physics for generations is probably correct. It also could be maintained that such a delay would have taken place if in the 1920s the University of Göttingen, birthplace of nuclear physics, had been blown up.

Whereas it is conceivable that universities, as communities of learning composed of students, faculty, and administrators, could be democratically organized, the reasons that speak against their being a rubberstamp of societies also speak against their democratic organization. Such an organization would interfere with the universities' paramount aim, the pursuit of the truth.

Beginners ought not to have as much to say as those who are older, more educated, and mature. Advanced students will generally feel superior to less advanced ones. A candidate for the doctorate is likely to resent a freshman's trying to run him, and rightly so.

The same applies *a fortiori* to the relationship between students and faculty. Permitting students an influence upon the formulation of academic policy would be tantamount to giving those with less knowledge and, therefore, less ability to advance the truth the same power as those who possess a greater knowledge and ability to do so. It would put men who have proved their excellence on a par with those who still must, and perhaps never will, prove it. Such a policy would topple the very tenets of education.

Within the faculty, there ought to be a strict distinction between assistants, assistant professors, associate professors, and professors. Since the selective process grows with learning, it can be less expected that full professors will consider themselves the equals of assistants or assistant professors than that seniors will consider themselves equal to freshmen or sophomores. While this is partly reflected in the fact that often only full professors are eligible for academic councils or senates and that their selection is restricted to their peers and perhaps associate professors, in general assemblies and departments all members often have an equal vote. While there is something to be said for that arrangement from the point of view of collegiality, it must never be forgotten that the universities' main aim is not collegiality, but excellence, and that the former might hurt the latter. Therefore, it might be advisable to weigh voting strength all the way through according to rank; to give, for instance, assistants 1 vote; assistant professors, 2; associate professors, 3; and professors, 4 votes.

Just as in the past decades the power of the faculty has increased for the sake of academic freedom, today we must emphasize, again for the sake of academic freedom, a strong administration. In view of the fact that faculty rather than administrators have been sympathetic to student behavior threatening academic freedom, the security of the university order in the present emergency probably is most safely vested in the administration and trustees. A greater centralization of power in these bodies would merely correspond to the concentration of government power in the hands of the executive in times of emergency. While such a concentration has, by no means, been without constitutional problems,[11] it has become quite generally accepted, even by the friends of constitutional government. It must be even more defensible if exercised by the rulers of universities who possess less compulsory power than their political counterparts.

Reason of university, then, not only entitles but

---

[11] Gottfried Dietze, *America's Political Dilemma* (1968), pp. 17 ff., 175 ff.

obligates the rulers of universities to do whatever is necessary for the free pursuit of the truth, provided they act in accordance with the laws and their contractual obligations. Since the devotion of students and faculty to academic freedom seems to have been decreasing, and since (perhaps also on account of the relatively large size and ensuing clumsiness of their bodies) they have failed to uphold that freedom in recent riots, that devotion must increase with the rulers who form a relatively small body that could more effectively combat challenges to the free university. Those rulers must look upon their position not as just another job carrying money and prestige, but as a calling for scholarship. As universities are struggling for their lives, those trusted with running them must pledge their lives to save them.

Whatever the commitments of the rulers of universities may be today, they must have, first of all, guts. Goodwill alone won't do. It must be accompanied by action. Whereas during the past decades military men were increasingly replaced by scholars as university presidents, the military men might now well be on their way back to replace intellectual nonheroes, who all too often have proved to be prone to commit *trahisons des clercs*. Just as university representatives in the past have not feared the power of popes, kings, and popular demagogues, they must today not be afraid of students, faculty, public opinion—or of their often powerful organizations. University representatives must be free men who are not impressed by blackmail and intimidation. Also, they must not be afraid of being called "illiberal." The latter attribute, if it comes from pseudoliberals who pay only lipservice to liberalism, ought to be considered a flattery rather than a reproach. In order to have the truth make us free, we must first be free to know the truth.[12]

As to university policy, we do not want here to write a Machiavellian treatise on how those in charge of universities should act. We merely suggest, for the present situation, a broad outline. A policy for reason of university would seem to fall into two major parts, that required for emergencies and that for combating the causes of campus unrest.

The principles that ought to govern emergencies are immediacy, severity, and consistency.

An emergency must be met by immediate counteraction. A riot is like a fire: unless put down right away, it spreads. The slower the reaction to it, the greater the harm. Berkeley, Columbia, and Cornell are cases in point. So are the Free University of Berlin and other German universities, where at one time the lady Rector of the University of Heidelberg put all her male colleagues to shame when, with a housewifely instinct, she alone took immediate action to save the situation by dissolving a student organization the way she might

---

[12] Gottfried Dietze, *Youth, University and Democracy* (1970), pp. 47 ff.

have trampled to death the mice in her pantry. If university regulations prescribe certain procedures for emergency measures (and such procedures ought not to be longwinded lest they frustrate immediate action), they ought to be followed. However, those procedures ought never to get in the way of a university executive should an emergency make immediate action imperative and if abiding by regulations would considerably worsen the situation. In that case, the executive must exercise the perogative of his office and act by decree.

Sanctions against the violators ought to be severe. Whenever applicable, violators should be punished according to criminal law. A better appreciation of what is lawful and unlawful can be expected of students than of other people in their age group. To prosecute the latter and not the former would be tantamount to punishing those who are less aware of their wrongdoing, rather than those who are more aware of it. Furthermore, those who generally profess to believe in egalitarianism and "social justice" ought not to claim privileges, for privilege is the enemy of justice. Last, but not least: Students, who as academic citizens belong to an elite, ought to be first, not last, in obeying the law. If student behavior is not punishable under criminal law, strict disciplinary sanctions ought to be applied, such as probation, suspension, and dismissal. In case of doubt, the sanctions should be harder rather than softer, in view of the fact that no disciplinary action is likely to cause real hardship. Even a dismissal does not prevent a violator from going somewhere else. It actually might be good for him, since, through his violations, he indicates that he finds fault with the university he is enrolled in. Of course, students should be held responsible for damages according to civil law.

Consistency must apply to the administration's emergency policy, to counteraction and sanctions. There ought to be no dillydallying with either, and no dilution of either. The administration must never leave the slightest doubt that it will not suffer any interruption of the regular process of learning. Once such an interruption occurs, emergency measures must be carried out consistently. There must never be given any indication that the administration might not be determined to fully restore an atmosphere conducive to free learning. There must be no stopping halfway, no willingness to compromise, if this would compromise the mission of the university. Sanctions against students, once applied, ought to be firmly carried out. Unless new evidence becomes known, there ought to be no commutation of penalties, lest the administration become the laughingstock of the community and encourage new threats to the university.

The principles which ought to govern the elimination of the causes of unrest are balance and excellence.

Since the causes of unrest have been due mainly to leftist activities, reason of university requires a curbing of leftists who, in many instances, act under the cover of academic freedom in order to undermine that freedom. This proposal should not be misunderstood. In spite of cogent doubts that have been raised about permitting those who want to destroy freedom to profit from it,[13] the freedom of teachers ought not to be curbed as long as it is used for rational discussion and does not reduce universities to political arenas. Rightists have as little a monopoly on the truth as leftists. But for this very reason, leftists ought not to act as they generally do today, as if they had such a monopoly, and, in the name of liberalism, condemn, ridicule, and ignore those who disagree with them. It would be best if the present preponderance of the left would prompt the faculty to restore a fair balance between modern and classic liberals and conservatives by hiring more of the latter.

Unfortunately, this kind of tolerance can seldom be found in faculties that generally discriminate against conservatives, especially in the social sciences. Therefore, the men ruling universities ought to assure a balance between various opinions, in order to make universities true marketplaces of ideas. They ought to hire more men tending toward the right and see to it that those already on the faculty suffer no disadvantages with respect to salary. This regrettable situation often exists today, largely because the conservatives' chances of getting offers from other institutions, overweighted as they generally are with leftists, are very

---

[13] Friedrich A. Hayek, *The Constitution of Liberty* (1960), pp. 390 ff.

slim, thus considerably reducing their bargaining power.

It goes without saying that a university must promote excellence not only by securing a balance of approaches and outlook, and thus making possible that clash of ideas which is so important for the stimulation of learning, but also by a more direct promotion of excellence. Such a promotion not only makes universities more immune to criticism, thus depriving those interested in campus unrest of local issues, but it is also likely to eliminate politics from the campus, because it is generally the failures in scholarship who turn to politicking. It is not necessary to discuss here the generally known aspects of excellence, but a few remarks on aspects that have come about with the expansion of universities, resulting from the requirements of mass education, are in order.

In an age of mass education, losing excellence seems to be about as easy as gaining leftists. Universities have been expanding their staffs in order to increase "depth." Actually, the staffs have expanded in width and quantity at the cost of depth and quality. This is unfortunate. Education through all is as bad as education for all. It tends to be no education at all. It is more important for universities to stay strong in fields where they have traditionally been strong than to add to their curriculum at the expense of the quality of the whole. In a situation that requires cutbacks, the elimination of new and weak departments might be advisable, especially so if these departments have attracted radicals that threaten the free pursuit of the truth and, thereby, excellence. It also is more important for the excellence of a university to have a few first-rate senior men who are leaders in their fields than to have many junior men who, it is hoped, will become such leaders and who all too often do not, instead becoming part of a growing academic proletariat that has consistently lowered the standards of higher education. Therefore, if cutbacks are necessary, junior men ought not to be kept, particularly in dubious cases, especially if keeping them means that senior men who retire would not be replaced by new senior men. Universities ought not to gamble with excellence. Again, the administration has to fulfill an important task in the pursuit of excellence. Faculties tend to hire, promote, and keep colleagues that are about as good as they are, rather than better. They tend to keep junior men whom they are used to, rather than take the trouble of looking around for others. The policy here proposed would also enable an administration to get rid of hotheads and sympathizers of radical students, who can most often be found among junior rather than senior faculty. A policy favoring excellence can thus be as conducive to the balance proposed in the preceding paragraph as that balance can aid excellence.[14]

---

[14] It will be argued that the policies here proposed imply hardship to part of the university community. This may well be true. How-

University of Reason and State of Reason

Our suggestions on what reason of university may require in the present situation are by no means exhaustive. What is to be done always depends upon the specific conditions in a specific university. Paraphrasing Meinecke again, we may continue the excerpt quoted in the beginning, saying that *raison d'université* indicates both the path and the goal for the growth of the university: "This path and this goal cannot be chosen quite at random; but neither can exactly the same ones be prescribed for all Universities. For the University is also an individual structure with its own characteristic way of life; and the laws general to the species are modified by a particular structural pattern and a particular environment. So the 'intelligence' of the University consists in arriving at a proper understanding both of itself and its environment, and afterwards in using this understanding to decide the principles which are to guide its behavior. These principles are always bound to be at the same time both individual and general, both constant and changeable. They will change subtly as alterations take place in the University itself and its environment. But they must also tally with what

---

ever, excellence cannot be achieved by supporting those who are not excellent. Welfare in the sense of the support of the mediocre is bad enough in a political society, whose major aim is convenience, because it aids the worst to get on top. It is even less defensible in a university, the aim of which must be excellence.

is lasting in the structure of the individual University, as well as with that which is permanent in the laws governing the life of all Universities. Thus from the realm of what is and what will be, there constantly emerges, through the medium of understanding, a notion of what ought to be and what must be. The ruler of the University *must,* if he is convinced of the accuracy of his understanding of the situation, act in accordance with it in order to reach his goal. The choice of path to the goal is restricted by the particular nature of the University and its environment. Strictly speaking, only one path to the goal (i.e., the best possible one at the moment) has to be considered at any one time. For each University at each particular moment there exists one ideal course of action, one ideal *raison d'université.*"[15]

In spite of their wide jurisdiction, the rulers of universities must not abuse their power and, especially in times of emergency when that power increases, always keep in mind Lord Acton's statement that "power tends to corrupt and absolute power corrupts absolutely."[16] They must be careful not to let measures in defense of the university degenerate into witch-hunting, and resist the temptation of excusing everything they do, even

---

[15] Meinecke, *Machiavellism,* p. 1.
[16] To Bishop Creighton on April 5, 1887. John N. Figgis and Reginald V. Lawrence (eds.), *Historical Essays and Studies* (1907), p. 504.

actions that are not warranted for the sake of the free exploration of the truth, for reason of university. Although Nietzsche perhaps wanted universities to take the place of churches, which in his opinion had failed to promote the truth, it must never be forgotten that, whereas professors should be priests of the truth protected by university rulers, universities are not churches. Universities are not organisms into which their members are born and from childhood on adjusted to certain ways of thinking and living. They are institutions that may have grown organically but are, nevertheless, based upon a contract freely concluded among thinking individuals conferring rights and duties upon the contracting partners. Therefore, the rulers of universities must never leave any doubt that their duty to aid free inquiry does not imply the right to act like grand inquisitors.

In the hopeful absence of an abuse of reason of university, the latter term, similar as it is to "reason of state," might actually be a misnomer. For, unlike reason of state, reason of university cannot be oppressive.[17]

The contractual character of the university community precludes that its members will suffer from reason of university the way citizens may suffer from reason of state, even under governments which provide for a far-reaching protection of the individual. One need not relegate the idea of the social contract to the

---

[17] Cf. *supra,* pp. 61 ff.

realm of fiction to realize that in today's societies based upon the contractual theory of government—not to mention those where that theory has been replaced by an organic one—citizens are born into the political community. By the sheer fact of birth, without their will, citizens automatically join a political organism of which, except for those who are permitted to emigrate, they remain a part for the rest of their lives, more or less willy-nilly. The society's government can force them to conform to its norms and sanction these norms by infringing upon their lives, liberty, and property.

On the other hand, often as proud parents may "register" the newly born at their alma mater, nobody becomes an academic citizen by birth. Those who enter a university do so of their own free will, usually after careful consideration and selection. They know what they are getting into, having received information concerning the university of their choice through catalogs and other means of orientation or, as in the case of faculty and administrators, through specific contracts. By registering or accepting the university's offer, academic citizens agree to the university order; i.e., its rules, regulations, and whatever may be required to uphold that order—including emergency measures for reason of university. It would be strange if someone who entered a university because its existence made him prefer it to other institutions would not want it to continue to exist. Since possible hardships for reason of university are permitted by the members of the academic community, and every member is free to leave that community at any time should he disagree with an aspect of university life, the hardships that some people tend to connect with the term "reason of university" cannot really be said to exist.

Even if those hardships existed, however, a policy for reason of university cannot be oppressive because it is pursued for the sake of the truth. For whatever is done for the exploration of the truth is done for the enlargement of freedom, whether we accept the connection between the truth and freedom in John 8:32, or that provided by the contemporary author of *Sein und Zeit*.[18] We must not only be free to know the truth, but the truth also makes us free.

The existence of universities has always required measures for reason of university, generally as a defense against measures for reason of state. Perhaps the need for reason of university increases with the scope of reason of state. In that case, there would be a strong need for reason of university in modern democracy, absolutist and majoritarian as the latter has become. Also, that need would be the smallest in a libertarian society, which considers that government best that governs least. In such a society, reason of state is likely to be minimal because state power, with all its political values and emotional trimmings, is reduced to a minimum and replaced by the "state of reason" (*Verstan-*

---

[18] Martin Heidegger, *Vom Wesen der Wahrheit* (3rd ed., 1954).

desstaat), which came to von Mohl's mind when he looked for a better name for *Rechtsstaat*.[19] As the state of reason is a state of rights, justice, law, and order, it also is a state of truth (*Wahrheitsstaat*) and freedom (*Freiheitsstaat*), a state whose values are likely to conform to the values of universities. In a state of reason, therefore, it can be expected that the doctrine of reason of university would fade away into a universality of reason in which the *universitas magistrorum et scholarium,* complemented by the *universitas scientiarum,* would, as a university of reason, no longer stand in need of reason of university.

---

[19] Robert von Mohl, *Das Staatsrecht des Königreiches Württemberg,* I (1829), p. 11.

The Revitalized College: A Model

Russell Kirk

Russell Kirk is the only American to hold the highest arts degree (earned) of the senior Scottish University—doctor of letters of St. Andrews. He obtained his bachelor's degree from Michigan State University and his master's from Duke University.

Dr. Kirk is the author of eighteen books, of which the most recent are Eliot and His Age *and* The Roots of American Order. *His best-known book,* The Conservative Mind, *first published in 1953, recently was reissued in a revised edition.*

He is editor of the quarterly University Bookman, *and consultant to several educational foundations and publishing firms. He has been professor of history, politics, and American studies at several universities and colleges, and has spoken on more than two hundred campuses. His syndicated column, "To the Point," distributed by the Los Angeles Times Syndicate, is published in more than a hundred daily newspapers.*

A few years ago, a graduate of New York University brought suit against that institution. He had been induced to enter those halls (so ran his plea) by the promise that through collegiate studies he would obtain wisdom. But after graduation, he found himself as ignorant as before; so he demanded his money back. I am sorry that the courts of New York did not find in his favor; had they done so, some reform of the higher learning in America might have commenced.

I have been asked to present to you a model for a good college of arts and sciences, regardless of whether there appears to be any possibility of such an institution being founded or renewed, and without concern for its prospects of survival, were it founded. Being no gnostic or utopian, and having in mind no Academy of Lagado, however, I venture to outline a reasonably practical scheme for such a college; a model of a college which *could* come into being, and *could* endure, under favorable circumstances. There exist historical, and indeed some extant, examples of what should be done; in an eclectic manner, I blend some of the virtues of those examples into my model. Change being the means of our preservation, I venture to suggest certain adaptations or improvements calculated to make the traditional American college relevant to the modern age. Bear with me, if you will.

The chief practical obstacle to the success of such a college as I have in mind (and you will understand that I am describing a college of arts and sciences, not a university with graduate faculties and facilities for research) is the low estate to which the American high school has fallen. Albert Jay Nock, in an exercise similar to mine, suggested once that before a really good college could commence its work, a sound high school—nay, primary and intermediate schools, too— must be founded, so that the students meant to enroll in the college might obtain adequate preparation, then and now available in very few schools. Surely that would be a mighty advantage for such a new college. Failing that, however, it might not be impossible to attract first-year college students of tolerably decent preparation by active seeking of them up and down the land; for as Nock (after Isaiah and Matthew Arnold) himself remarked in a different essay of his, there exists always a Remnant, more numerous than any prophet thinks possible, who will hearken to a clear call and promise. A portion of that educational Remnant, aged seventeen or eighteen years, would suffice to form a hopeful first-year class, for the number ought to be kept small. (As Lord Percy of Newcastle wrote, it is not good to be educated in a crowd.)

Since I am not required to remain within the frontiers of the realm of the possible, however, let me pass from such considerations to concerns more theoretical. I propose first of all to suggest the chief end of such a model college of arts and sciences; next to consider the chief approaches to that end; then to discuss the failings, and the hopes for regeneration, within existing colleges; finally, to offer certain concrete proposals for the general frame and conduct of that model college.

Wisdom as the End

We must begin with first principles, which sound platitudinous. We need to recall, nevertheless, that platitudes are *true:* that is why they have become platitudes. What, then, is the chief end of a college of arts and sciences? Why, to enable a body of senior scholars (the professors) and a body of junior scholars (the undergraduates) to seek after Wisdom—and through Wisdom, for Truth.

The end is not success, pleasure, or sociability, but wisdom. This wisdom is not the same as facts, utility, training, or even knowledge. No college can confer wisdom, but a good college can help its members to acquire the means to pursue wisdom. Wisdom means apprehension of the human condition, recognition of reality, and the experience and possession of high knowledge—together with the power to apply experience and knowledge critically and practically. Although it is still relatively easy to find learned fools, true wisdom is rare; and so must wisdom always be. Still, in the hope that wisdom may not be extinguished altogether in our generation, I endeavor to present to you a model college that might help to make the acquisition of wisdom less difficult than it is at present; a college some of whose graduates might be philosophers (lovers of wisdom), and many of whose graduates might be, at least, men of right reason, humane inclinations, and sound taste.

There have been such colleges. One (somewhat before my time) was St. Stephen's College—now called Bard College—at Annandale-on-Hudson, when the late Dr. Bernard Iddings Bell was president. He was a good president, as good presidents go. And as good presidents go, he went—and the model college went with him. The Gadarene swine never rooted more widely than they do in our age. Yet we must not despair.

For a literary model of such a college dedicated to *veritas*—to the pursuit of that wisdom which recognizes enduring truth—we do well to turn to the writings of John Henry Newman. The best known of these is Newman's *The Idea of a University;* the most moving, his discourse "What Is a University?" in *The Office and Work of Universities*. Of course, Newman was describing a university with several faculties, not a liberal college merely; but most of what he wrote may be applied to our present concern. His university never took on flesh: the Ireland of his day was not ready for it, and Ireland seems to be less ready now. Here, however that may be, we are discussing what is desirable, not what is immediately practicable.

Newman emphasized that the aim of the formal higher learning is cultivation of the intellect for the intellect's own sake. (In his Irish circumstances at that time it was necessary that he emphasize the claims of the intellect, for the Irish bishops, fearing the modern mind, were all too ready to settle for faith and morals, looking upon the projected university merely as an enlarged seminary.) Yet if we look at Newman's work in general, we come to understand that by "intellect" or "knowledge" he meant no narrow rationalism. He knew that the fear of God is the beginning of wisdom; he knew, too, that a primary purpose of the higher learning is to develop the moral imagination; he understood that reason may be baneful unless it is dedicated to an ethical end. I do not think that Newman would disagree overmuch with my own object for a true college education. I hold that the higher learning is an intellectual means to an ethical end; that the college is meant to join knowledge with virtue, so helping to develop persons who enjoy some wisdom because they subordinate private rationality to the claims of what T. S. Eliot called "the permanent things." The means must be strictly and rigorously intellectual; the end must be ethical, in that right reason is employed to attain moral worth.

In fine, I recommend a restoration of genuinely liberal education within which the natural sciences, in their philosophical sense, are comprehended. By a liberal discipline, says Newman in the fifth discourse of *The Idea of a University,* "A habit of mind is formed which lasts throughout life, of which the attributes are, freedom, equitableness, calmness, moderation, and wisdom; or what in a former discourse I have ventured to call the philosophical habit." We should not claim too much for such a discipline: "Its direct business is not to steel the soul against temptation or to console it in affliction, any more than to set the loom in motion, or to direct the steam carriage; be it ever so much the means or the condition of both material and moral advancement, still, taken by and large, it as little mends our hearts as it improves our temporal circumstances." It cannot directly instill virtue: "Quarry the granite rock with razors, or moor the vessel with a thread of silk; then you may hope with such keen and delicate instruments as human knowledge and human reason to contend against those giants, the passion and the pride of man." At its best, it remains a method, a discipline, for teaching the mind right reason and modesty of intellectual aspiration. "A young man of sharp and active intellect, who has had no other training, has little to show for it besides a litter of ideas heaped up into his mind any how." So Newman writes in his *Lectures and Essays on University Subjects.*

Not learning or acquirement, but thought or reason exercised upon knowledge, is the end of intellectual training. The real aim of education, Newman declares, is "the clear, calm, accurate vision and comprehension of all things, as far as the finite mind can embrace them, each in its place, and with its own characteristics upon it." Amen to that. What higher education, in its formal sense, can accomplish is limited. But if it can confer, or help to confer, this wise vision, it will have done much to enable a man to order his own soul and, thereby, come to a condition of moral worth. And by doing that, it will have contributed mightily toward order in the commonwealth.

Liberal Learning, Moral Worth, and Defecated Rationality

T. S. Eliot, lecturing in 1950 at the University of Chicago on "The Aims of Education," made many wise observations, one of which may serve as my apology for discussing the management of American colleges, a work in which I have had little experience.* "It seems to me that it is the task of educators to think and write

---

* Eliot's Chicago lectures later were published in his collection *To Criticize the Critic* (New York: Farrar, Straus & Giroux, Inc., 1965).

about education," Eliot remarked, "but to clarify for themselves the social, philosophical, and theological presuppositions which underlie their generalizations; and it is for the pure theoretician, the philosopher or theologian, to refer his theories to the educator—the man who has had experience of the difficulties of teaching anybody anything." I write here as one of those theoreticians, although not, I hope, as one of Burke's abstract metaphysicians, whose hearts were so consummately wicked.

My thesis is this: a principal achievement of liberal education in America has been the imparting of a sense of moral worth among those who lead intellectually. This apprehension of moral worth, as taught by the liberal disciplines, has been losing ground, throughout the present century, to what Newman called the "Knowledge School"—that is, to utilitarian and pragmatic theories and practices, which tend to regard moral worth (so far as they regard it at all) as merely the product of private rationality and social utility. Success, increasingly, has been substituted for virtue in our curricula; facts, for wisdom; social adjustment, for strength of soul. What, in certain books of mine, I have called "defecated rationality" (that is, the petty bank and capital of private rationality, as distinguished from the wisdom of our ancestors, religion, custom, convention, reverence, and honor) nowadays is generally considered the brightest gem in a scholar's crown. And if this latter-day view of the ends of education is carried to its logical culmination, we must efface the principle which for three centuries has breathed life into the unwieldy bulk of our system of higher education.

I do not perceive any practical substitute being offered for this old sustaining principle. Therefore, I recommend that we do whatever is in our power to restore a general consciousness that the aim of higher education is the inculcation of an understanding of moral worth, achieved through right reason. Without a proper understanding of moral worth, there is little point in talking about human dignity, education for democracy, adjustment to modern society, training for leadership, preparation for the modern world, or pointing the way to success. For what gives a man dignity, what makes possible a democracy of elevation, what makes any society tolerable, what gives leaders their right to office, what keeps the modern world from becoming *Brave New World,* and what constitutes real success in any walk of life is the attainment of moral worth.

Our colleges cannot undertake the whole task of conveying to the rising generation an understanding of moral worth. If a student comes to college with no morals or (what is much the same thing) with bad morals, it is improbable that the college can do much to improve his understanding of moral worth, whatever it may do for his sheer intellectuality. The mission of the college is to reconcile moral principle with right reason, rather than to undertake some eleventh-hour program of ethical exhortation. What a college can do, nevertheless, is to remind its students that intellectual achievement and moral worth are not incompatible, and that intellectual attainment does not grant to young people a license of emancipation from the claims of moral worth.

I am inclined to agree with Socrates that virtue cannot be taught. Such is the conclusion to which that philosopher comes in the course of conversations with his disciples. Yet Socrates was a great moralist; his aim was to make philosophy an ethical study once more, rescuing it from the pit of abstract speculation, on the one hand, and from the slough of the sophistical pursuit of power and success on the other. Virtue cannot be taught formally and abstractly. Yet, Socrates and his pupils agree, the wise man is the good man, and the good man is the wise man. I do not propose to pursue here the various merits and difficulties of this latter doctrine. I am only pointing out that Socrates believed the end of learning to be ethical, and that right reason would support the cause of virtue; yet he thought that the identification of the virtuous life with the wise life was to be attained by indirection and subtle processes, rather than by formal indoctrination. Nor was Socrates unaware that intellectuality of a high order, if undirected by conscience or habit, may lead men into evil courses—indeed, into consummate folly. Socrates' daemon is a guide to private reason and yet a

prompter (like conscience or an "inner check") somehow above and beyond private judgment and immediate motive. In Plato's *Apology,* when Socrates was
confronted with the charge that Alcibiades and Critias,
among his pupils, had not been eminent examples of
moral worth, he implied that there are men whose light
is darkness, and whom no teacher may improve morally, no matter how much he may sharpen their rational
faculties.

Thus it is with our colleges. They cannot make
vicious students virtuous or stupid students wise. They
can, however, endeavor to prove to their students that
intellectual power is not hostile toward moral worth,
and they can aspire to chasten intellectual presumption. In his first discourse on the idea of a university,
Newman makes it clear that the higher learning improves intellects, rather than consciences. Yet Newman's was a profoundly ethical concept of higher
education, with theology reigning supreme over all
studies. I repeat that the college's ultimate achievement
is moral, but that its method is intellectual. And at no
time is the work of a college purely intellectual or yet
purely moral.

We cannot set up a course of instruction called
"Moral Worth 101" and expect to confer upon students, along with three credits, an apprehension of
what man is and wherein his duties lie and in what his
dignity consists. Far more than through formal instruction or through processes directly rational, we learn

through the faculty that Newman calls "the illative sense"—illation, the eductive process, rather than the institutionalized educational process. Colleges cannot adequately compensate for deficiencies in the understanding of moral worth in the family, in the church, in the elementary schools, or in society at large. Nor do formally schooled persons enjoy any monopoly of the appreciation of moral worth. Prejudice and prescription, by which "a man's virtue becomes his habit," can and often do make the unlettered man as morally worthy as the scholar, or make him even the scholar's moral superior. Yet I believe that if the intellectual leaders of a society deny the value of traditional morality, or are ignorant of that morality, then the mass of men will not long remain obedient to the moral dictates of prejudice and prescription. I do not ask, then, that our colleges should undertake the task of moral instruction directly, or assume burdens which other organs of society ought to perform. I am asking only that our colleges should acknowledge the primacy of moral worth, and that they should not set their faces against moral learning as being somehow archaic, authoritarian, and unscientific.

Unaided, our colleges cannot restore or maintain among us the concept of human dignity, as expressed in standards of moral principle. But our colleges do possess the negative power of discrediting the whole idea of human dignity by consigning the great intellectual tradition of moral worth as the crown of wisdom—that belief which inspired the Roman *humanitas* and which obtained fuller expression in Christian teaching—to the Kingdom of the Fairies, along with some other old notions presumably exploded.

I am afraid that some educators have been working this rejection in words, if not in deeds. They have been ready to profess that defecated rationality is better than moral authority or that success, adjustment, and positivistic social improvement (rather than imparting of moral imagination) are the only concerns of an institution of higher learning. If they accomplish this rejection generally, they will alienate themselves from the principal achievement of higher education in America, and will expose us all to the probability of an accelerated decline of American thought, character, and public order.

Among democratic peoples, Alexis de Tocqueville writes in the second volume of *Democracy in America,* materialism is a disease particularly dangerous. "Democracy encourages a taste for physical gratification; this taste, if it becomes excessive, soon disposes men to believe that all is matter only; and materialism, in its turn, hurries them on with mad impatience to these same delights; such is the fatal circle within which democratic nations are driven round."

In the past, American colleges often strove to hold us back from that fatal circle. They clung, however feebly, to Newman's conviction that literature and science, unaided, cannot give the answers to the great questions of modern life. They were, in some degree, conservators of moral worth. My model college would renew that function; indeed, would fulfill it more adequately than it was fulfilled in the past.

Colleges have been drifting away from their old moral and intellectual purposes. They have been accepting assimilation to what is called "business civilization"; or devoting themselves to training an intellectual and technological elite intended to govern some future gorgeous domination; or employing their facilities to teach the notion that "everybody belongs to everybody else." It is high time to revitalize the college. "What irony there would be in having learned to control matter," George Santayana writes, "if we thereby forgot the purposes of the mind, our sense, fancy, and pictorial knowledge." It would be still more ironic if, in the triumph of organization and technology, we should forget the understanding of moral worth, achieved through an intellectual process.

Prudent change is the means for conserving the continuity of any institution. Whether that prudent change ought to be "forward," in a bold new direction, or "backward," to a restoration of old essentials neglected, depends upon particular circumstances and the temper of the age. In general, our society seems to require a reform that is reactionary, rather than innovating. For while there is little risk that our generation may cease to hanker after new things, there exists danger that our generation, or at least the rising generation, may break the contract of eternal society, forgetting that we are wise in our generation only because our modern intellectual edifices rest upon ancient foundations, the moral and intellectual achievements of our ancestors. Those who ignore the past, as Santayana says, are condemned to repeat it. But also, understanding the past of the American college, we should find it possible in a model college to work certain improvements over the college of a century ago, say.

I think that the peculiar conditions of our time and our society demand now, more than ever before, a reinvigoration of truly liberal learning. This hour is favorable to the restoration or establishment of a college with principle. A representative of a charitable foundation once observed to me that any college that believes in anything still is in a state comparatively healthy, so far as support goes, no matter how silly or how sound that particular belief of the college may be. If that college clearly has faith in orthodox Christianity, in militant atheism, in oldfangled *laissez-faire,* in revisionist socialism, or in some venerable discipline of the mind, then that college does not lack for a vigorous faculty, a lively student body, or a generous group of patrons. Commitment to principle brings success as a by-product. And my own visits to several hundred campuses, over the years, tend to confirm that gentleman's thesis.

Most colleges today, however, seem terrified of commitment to principle; indeed, they seem opposed to principles on principle. Their trustees and presidents and professors tend to think of doubt as a good in itself, of "ambivalence" as identical with the liberal understanding, and of faith as bigotry. Thus, those colleges are left with merely quantitative standards or (at best) a vague aestheticism. What a rudder in a sea of troubles!

It is the college that can boast justifiably of its commitment to principle and of its high standards and its humane scale which will attract the better senior scholars, the better junior scholars, and the benefactions of industry, the foundations, and the private patron. The college can survive and prosper not by imitating the mass-schooling methods of Brummagem University but by offering a discipline of intellect, ethical in aim, which mass education neglects. So permit me to suggest succinctly how the typical American college has gone astray before I proceed to some regenerative recommendations.

Decline and Survival

The aim of the oldfangled college education was ethical, the development of moral understanding and of humane leadership; but the method was intellectual, the training of mind and conscience through well-defined literary disciplines. A college was an establishment for the study of important literature. It was nearly that simple.

Through an apprehension of great literature, young men were expected to fit themselves for leadership in the churches, in the law, in politics, in principal positions of public responsibility. This was what the late Gordon Chalmers (after Sir Thomas Elyot) called "the education of governors." Whatever the faults of this system, it did produce a body of sound-principled and literate men to be the leaders of the American democracy. They learned to govern themselves and to serve the republic, through strict attention to great literature: the poetry, philosophy, and history of Greece and Rome, especially; the Bible, with the history of the Jews; something of modern thought and languages; and something of the literature of science. The subjects of study were few, and the course of study was uniform.

The intention of the college was not to confer a vague smattering of every branch of knowledge upon its students, but rather to teach students the fundamental disciplines to logical thought, provide them with a taste and a critical faculty for independent reading and meditation, and then send them into the world with a cast of character and mind fitted for ethical and intellectual leadership. If these young persons remembered no more from college than something of Biblical history and precepts from Cicero and episodes from Plutarch (and some young men retained a great deal besides), still that knowledge prepared them better for life (the life of their time or of ours) than does the cafeteria-curriculum of many universities and colleges nowadays, whose graduates may not open a single important book after they have snatched their diplomas.

Most surviving American colleges fail to achieve this fairly modest goal because they try to be all things to all men. They promise what they cannot perform, and never could perform. They promise to teach adjustment to the group, social polish, sociability, trades, salesmanship, business acumen, and the art of worldly wisdom —or what you will. They ape the functions of the universities and of the technical schools. With murmured apology and shamefacedness, they consign to a dusty corner of the curriculum their old disciplines; when, that is, they do not abolish altogether the classics, humane letters, languages, moral philosophy, and speculative science. Those arts that teach us what it is to be a man are thrust aside by business science, communications skills, journalism, premedicine, rudimentary sociology, and even "pop culture." Most of the colleges have abandoned their ethical end and forgotten their intellectual means. The wonder is not that the colleges are in difficulties, but that they survive at all. For when function ceases, form atrophies.

Certain things a college can do very well. It can give the student the tools for educating himself throughout his life. It can present to him certain general principles for the governance of personality and community. It can help him to see what makes life worth living. It can teach him basic disciplines which will be of infinite value in professional specialization at a university or in his subsequent apprenticeship to any commercial or industrial occupation.

And certain things no honest college can pretend to do at all. It cannot teach the student directly to win friends and influence people. It cannot make him a successful captain of industry, an accomplished engineer, or a specialized scientist. It cannot guarantee him worldly prosperity. It cannot simply enroll him in a survey course in "world culture" and pour the milk of learning into him.

Now it is quite possible that a person who has been immersed in the pseudoschooling and the vocational shams of a corrupted college may enjoy a considerable measure of practical success and, at the same time, be an intelligent and honest man. Two friends of mine, who attend the college that I did, there majored in journalism. One can no more really learn the craft of journalism in college than one really can learn the craft of whaling from reading *Moby Dick*. One may acquire in college, indeed, a knowledge of what current events mean, from studies in history, or some aptitude for writing from steady practice at preparing papers for various courses. But "majoring in journalism" has nothing to do with this. My two friends, despite their college curriculum, came to read good books and fill responsible positions: one a chief project engineer at an automobile factory, the other chief underwriter of an insurance firm. They redeemed themselves from the faults of their formal education and, for that matter, learned a good deal during their college years—but not from the vocational training they fondly embraced. The "useful" knowledge, the "practical" instruction, is obsolete almost before the student enters the busy world. A college wastes its resources and its students' time when it pretends to teach what can be taught only in workaday life, in the trade school, or in the graduate school.

What the college actually ought to do, and can do, was expressed forcefully by Irving Babbitt in a book published at the beginning of this century, *Literature and the American College*. (The study of enduring literature, I repeat, is the primary instrument of college education. When British universities used to consider the possibility of some new chair, they put to themselves this essential question, "To what body of literature does the proposed course of study refer?" Babbitt, then, was not writing merely of courses in the poetry of Keats and Shelley when he gave his little book its title.)

"The best of the small colleges," Babbitt wrote, "will render a service to American education if they decide to make a sturdy defense of the humane tradition instead of trying to rival the great universities in displaying a full line of educational novelties. In the latter case, they may become third-rate and badly equipped scientific schools, and so reenact the fable of the frog that tried to swell itself to the size of an ox. . . . Even though the whole world seems bent on living the quantitative life, the college should remember that its business is to make of its graduates men of quality in the real and not the conventional meaning of the term. In this way it will do its share toward creating that aristocracy of character and intelligence which is needed in a community like ours to take the place of an aristocracy of birth, and to counteract the tendency toward an aristocracy of money."

Throughout the past seventy years, the average American college has disregarded Babbitt's admonition, pleading that the college must give the public what the public seems to demand. But now the time is upon us when the college can and must heed the principles which Babbitt himself so well exemplified. The vast state-supported institutions have so thoroughly yielded to the presumed "public demand" for specialization, vocationalism, and intellectual egalitarianism that even the most complaisant liberal-arts college can no longer compete successfully with its enormous subsidized rivals for the favors of those students who desire, or think they desire, a shallow veneer of "culture," a trade-school discipline with a college diploma, and four years of idleness. If the private college competes with the state-supported institution along those lines, the college will succeed in enrolling only those students who fail to meet even the relaxed academic requirements of the state-supported institutions. And no one is going to be passionately interested in keeping alive a college that has become not much better than an intellectual bargain basement stuffed with rejects from the upper floors.

So I set down here, tentatively, some general principles by which colleges might begin to resume their old function—and perhaps to improve upon their old performance. To clothe these principles with flesh would require some courage of the people responsible for a college's policies. But one has to begin somewhere. The American college cannot afford much longer to drift with the current of events. Out of urgent necessity, if from no higher motive, the college policymakers may begin to reexamine the ends and means of a college education.

1. The college should reaffirm that the end of a liberal education is an ethical consciousness, through which the student is brought to an apprehension of the enduring truths that govern our being, of the principles of self-control, and of the dignity of man.

2. The college should make it clear that this ethical end is sought through an intellectual discipline, exacting in its character, which regards "useless knowledge" as infinitely more valuable than simple utilitarian skills.

3. The college should return to a concise curricu-

lum emphasizing religious knowledge, moral philosophy, humane letters, rhetoric, languages, history, logic, and the pure sciences.

4. The college should set its face against amorphous "survey courses," "general education," and similar substitutes for really intellectual disciplines. Such a smattering produces only that little learning which is a dangerous thing.

5. The college should turn away from vocationalism, resigning to trade schools and industrial "in-service training" what the college never was founded to undertake.

6. The college should abandon its attempt to encroach upon the specialized and professional studies which are the proper province of the graduate schools of universities.

7. The college should say less about "socialization" and "personality building" and more about the improvement of the human reason, for the human reason's own sake.

8. The college should give up as lost endeavor its aspiration to attract those students who desire the "extra-curricular benefits" of Behemoth University, and offer instead its own natural advantages of personal relationships, smallness of scale, and respect for individuality.

9. The college should not content itself with enrolling those students who cannot obtain entrance to a large university or state college. On the

contrary, it should begin to set its standards higher than those of Behemoth University.

10. The college should endeavor deliberately to keep its student body within reasonable limits, its humane scale being one of its principal virtues.

11. The college should emancipate itself from quasi-commercialized programs of athletics, an expensive and often anti-intellectual pastime in which it cannot compete successfully with Behemoth University.

12. The college should reduce to a minimum the elective feature in its curriculum, for one of the college's principal strengths was formerly its recognition of order and hierarchy in the higher learning, and the undergraduate ordinarily is not yet capable of judging with discretion what his course of studies ought to be.

13. The college should recollect the importance of furnishing society with a body of tolerably well-schooled persons whose function it is to provide right reason and conscience in the commonwealth.

14. The college should inculcate in its students a sense of gratitude toward the generations that have preceded us in time and a sense of obligation toward the generations yet to be born. It should remind the rising generation that we are part of a long continuity and essence, and that

we moderns are only dwarfs standing upon the shoulders of giants. This consciousness lies at the heart of a liberal education.

Cheerfulness and Practicality Break in

Canon Bernard Iddings Bell once was showing an English visitor about the environs of Chicago. They drove past a handsome Gothic building of stone. "Is that a school?" inquired the visitor.

"Yes—a new one, 'distressed' to appear old," Canon Bell replied.

"Indeed! Who is the headmaster?"

"There is no headmaster."

"Curious! A kind of soviet of teachers, I suppose."

"There are no masters at all."

"Really? Then where are the boys?"

"As yet, there are no students. Here in the United States, we proceed educationally in a way to which you are unaccustomed," Canon Bell told his friend. "First we erect a building; then we obtain students; next we recruit teachers; then we find a headmaster; and at last we determine what is to be taught. You begin at the other end in England."

Let it be otherwise with our model college. The first matter to determine is the program of study, some outlines of which I already have suggested, but which will bear more detailed examination. After that, let us turn to the staff, then to the students, and finally to the "plant."

The Curriculum

The curriculum ought to be designed to rouse the moral imagination: to impart an apprehension of reality through studies which concern the nature of man and the condition in which we find ourselves, it being understood that man is a moral being—the only conscious creature—in whose existence greatness and misery are blended. These studies should be genuine intellectual disciplines, not "surveys" or "rap sessions" or courses of ideological exhortation. You will recall that in our model college, we assume that the undergraduates will be capable of some serious intellectual endeavor, having obtained a decent schooling before they enroll.

There should be only a few subjects taught, but those should be taught thoroughly and well. It would be best to have no one enroll in more than three courses each term. The college year should consist of six months only, after the Scottish fashion. In the month-long vacations at Christmas and Easter, and during summer, the students would have opportunity (and probably necessity) for independent reading, travel, and discussion among themselves.

The primary disciplines ought to be moral philosophy (not the fashionable logical positivism), history, humane letters (to develop critical power, not mere "appreciation"), rhetoric (perhaps combined with humane letters), political economy (not the amorphous "sociology" and "social science" which afflict most colleges nowadays), physics and higher mathematics (these being most important nowadays for developing the philosophical habit), biological science (also philosophically considered), classical and modern languages, and music and the visual arts (these last being historical and theoretical studies, rather than crafts). Other chairs or subjects might be added, depending upon resources, but they ought not to be added if that would reduce attention to the primary disciplines.

Within these several fields, proliferation of course offerings and intensive specialization of courses ought to be discouraged. There ought to be taught methods of approach to a scholarly discipline, rather than masses of information. Specialization may be arranged *within* a general course, according to the talents and interests of professor and student.

It probably would be unwise to have a separate "department of religion"; the study of religion would occur within the several disciplines, systematic theology and the like being left to separate theological schools. But the whole curriculum, in the phrase of Dr. Philip Phenix, should be "suffused with reverence."

A bachelor's degree should be awarded at the end of three years, not four. Perhaps an additional year of study, more specialized, would bring an additional honors degree. Tests and examinations should be reduced to a minimum, perhaps only at the end of an academic year, but then thorough and severe. Those failing would be permitted to take a similar examination before the beginning of the autumn term of the next academic year; those still failing then would be dismissed from the college.

Instruction ordinarily should be by formal lecture, well prepared. The students would be expected to read thoroughly, far beyond the crib called a textbook. Any professor or instructor whose lectures might be merely the equivalent of a standard textbook would be summarily dismissed. A tutorial system would be adopted, permitting frequent conferences between tutors and undergraduates, and private programs of reading and paper-writing. This is very expensive; but we are discussing the *model* college.

The Staff

The staff should be engaged upon the basis of learning and liveliness, regardless of degrees. Experience of the world, or personal achievement in a particular field, ought often to be given preference over a doctoral degree from a university with prestige, or over a long list of specialized publications.

Every member of the staff should enjoy a high degree of freedom in his own approach to instruction, it being clearly understood that he is to teach an intellectual discipline, not some impassioned private *doxa*. In a first-year course in history, for instance, he might devote the lecture period to an examination of a particular historical period or problem, thus teaching the historical *method* and leaving historical narrative to the investigation of the students, a great number of books being available to them.

Management of the college's academic affairs should be in the hands of a college senate, in large part. Deans might be chosen by that senate from regular members of the staff, to serve for only a year or two, more or less in rotation. The president might be chosen by the regents or trustees from a number of persons placed in nomination by the senate, ordinarily. This, like other matters touched upon here, is suggested upon the assumption that professors and instructors will be temperate and prudent people chosen only after deliberation.

Only one series of formal lecture classes should be required each year of senior members of the staff, at least; but much time will be spent in tutorial consultations.

The Students

The students should be admitted upon the basis of genuine intellectual interest and tolerable preparation; they should be made to understand that they are partners in a real educational enterprise, but junior partners. Although serious educational deficiencies would be a bar to admittance to this college, it is unnecessary (indeed, undesirable) that all students should be sobersidedly and consciously intellectual; nor need students necessarily place high on standard admissions tests, have been in the first rank at secondary schools, or furnish proof of possessing some astounding intelligence quotient. What matter most are intellectual liveliness, application to studies, and literary competence.

To assure that students' interests are adequately represented, it might be well for them to elect, annually or for a term of two or three years, a rector, after the pattern of the Scottish universities. Ideally, this representative (exercising almost the power of the tribune in the faculty senate, if need be) should be a gentleman and a scholar of mature years, chosen from outside the college, and willing to serve actively. Often a man of some distinction, retired from public affairs, might be found to stand for election to this office by the students.

Numerous scholarships, awarded without regard to students' individual means, ought to be available. Tuition and fees ought to be kept low, in part through endowments, in part through economical use of the college's funds: the elimination of costly athletic programs, abstinence from grandiose educational designs, reduction of course offerings, and prejudice against bricks-and-mortar expansion. Also it would be well to encourage, and perhaps to arrange, programs for long-term loans to students, through which they could repay to the college or to a bank, after graduation, the equivalent of their cost of instruction.

The "Plant"

The college's buildings should be handsome and permanent, but not luxurious. The campus should not resemble a public park or a fun fair: the more cloistered, the better. The administration building should be as small and uncomfortable as possible, to dishearten educational bureaucracy.

Under present circumstances, the college should not enter the housing business, except possibly for residences for some of the professors. Unless the college is isolated, there should be little or no provision of dormitories. Residential fraternities are to be encouraged in some circumstances, however, and should work out satisfactorily, supposing that the college attracts the sort of student described earlier. Similarly, the college should leave food catering to private enterprise, ordinarily. The doctrine of *in loco parentis* should be abandoned, for the most part. Despite this college's dedication to the idea of moral worth and its emphasis upon the moral imagination, the college is engaged in the improvement of intellects, not the immediate cure of souls. (Any students with psychiatric problems should transfer to another sort of institution, or else obtain assistance privately.) Students who commit unlawful acts, however, or those who systematically endeavor to impede the functioning of the college, should be promptly dismissed.

The first building to be erected (supposing that a college must be built, rather than reformed or acquired by reformers) should be the faculty club or commons, to promote the development of genuine community among the senior scholars and to assure them of the respect in which they are held. Around that center the college could develop, intellectually and physically. (After more than a century of existence, many American colleges and universities still have no faculty gathering place.)

The second building to be erected should be the library, which need not be vast, but which should be a careful collection, with adequate provision of serious periodicals. There should be easy access to the books at all reasonable hours, and the place should not be overheated.

The third building to be erected should be a chapel (whether or not the college has church sponsorship); I put this third only because the faculty commons or the library might be used for such purposes until the college has a body of undergraduates.

The fourth building to be erected should be one of lecture halls. There need not be extravagant provision of lecture halls and classrooms, because on most American campuses nowadays, through inefficient schedul-

ing, there is much waste of classroom space; and there
will be fewer classes held at this model college than at
the typical American college.

Other buildings will be added, of course. The campus
should be compact, the buildings harmonious, and the
whole should present the appearance of a distinct, self-
contained academic community. It is of the first importance *not* to employ an architect accustomed to
designing public schools. There should be a number of
pleasant, quiet gathering places or study retreats out
of doors.

One more note: this should be a segregated college
—by sex. There might be a model college for men and
a model college for women, perhaps not far distant
from each other. But one thing to avoid is the dating-
and-mating pattern which obsesses the typical American institution of a learning allegedly higher. Wine and
beer should be readily available to students in public
places, where that is not in conflict with local statutes,
and in fraternities and residence halls, on Chesterton's
principle that beer does more than Milton can to justify
God's ways to man. Recurrent disorderly conduct,
however, should not be tolerated; and, of course, any
user of narcotics should be expelled, as should any
student who engages in cheating or other dishonorable
activity. The students will be presumed to be men, not
boys, intellectually and emotionally. If they do not
justify that assumption, they must go elsewhere. This
campus would be a sanctuary for academic leisure, but

not a sanctuary for the fanatic, the criminal, or the psychotic.

Here I have offered merely the bare bones of a model, deliberately inviting full discussion; others may clothe this skeleton with flesh, or with draperies from the wardrobe of a moral imagination. I do not expect that this model college, if ever established, would supplant Behemoth University, even though Behemoth University (and Brummagem University) is far gone in decadence. This model college has no mission to the masses whose parents desire snob-degrees and sham-degrees for their progeny. My only hope is that we might thus leaven the lump of our present unappetizing educational dough. For those intelligent students now deeply discontented with the pabulum they are fed, this model college might be a vision come true; for those senior scholars who still earnestly stand by the works of the mind, and who desire to communicate what they know to the rising generation, this model college might be as attractive as All Souls' College. A college of this sort, governed by the traditions of reverence, learning, and civility, goes directly against the grain of present-day American education. But I attest the rising generation.

Essay Three

The Political Economy
of Modern Universities

Henry G. Manne

Henry G. Manne received his B.A. degree from Vanderbilt University in 1950, his J.D. from the University of Chicago Law School in 1952, his LL.M. in 1953 and S.J.D. in 1966 from Yale University Law School. He is a member of Phi Beta Kappa, Order of the Coif, and the Mont Pelerin Society. He was a member of the faculty of the law schools of St. Louis University, the University of Wisconsin, and George Washington University prior to assuming his present position as William R. Kenan, Jr., Professor of Law, Department of Political Science, University of Rochester. Professor Manne has been a Visiting Professor at U.C.L.A., the University of Michigan, and Stanford Law Schools. He is the author of Insider Trading in the Stock Market *(1966) and (with Henry Wallich)* The Modern Corporation and Social Responsibility *(1973), and editor of* Economic Policy and the Regulation of Corporate Securities *(1969); and has also written numerous articles and papers in popular and scholarly journals. He is a member of the Illinois and New York and U.S. Supreme Court Bars.*

Introduction

An attempt will be made in this paper to examine the modern private university from an organization theory approach. The organizational arrangements of the modern university will be analyzed in an effort to explain the behavior of various individuals connected with these institutions. The list of characters includes trustees, administrators, faculty, graduate students, and undergraduates. The approach of this paper is somewhat different from that of related works by such authors as Ben Rogge, Armen Alchian, and James Buchanan. These authors have focused on the economic effects of less-than-full-cost tuition, and, while many of their points will be touched upon in this paper, the principal focus here is somewhat broader.

The theme of this paper is that the nonprofit organization of universities is probably the principal determinant of less-than-full-cost tuition, with all its implications, and also of many other aspects of university life. Hopefully, this broader approach will explain a wider range of issues and behavior patterns that can be related exclusively to the less-than-full-cost tuition circumstance.

No effort will be made to examine in detail the full behavioral implications of state-owned and state-operated universities, though the development of state universities, it will be argued, played an important role in establishing some aspects of the modern private university. Obviously, there are a number of similarities between the two, but these extrapolations will be left to the reader.

This paper is offered in some respects as a complex hypothesis about universities rather than as an absolute proof of the propositions offered. To this end some historical developments in the American university scene will be sketched, but only to serve certain analytical purposes. No historical research has been done on the development of American universities, and, for the most part, conjecture about that development is offered here rather than hard data. Nonetheless, the broad outlines of that development are well enough known that any errors in this regard should not affect the analysis significantly.

Origins of Modern Organizational Form

Until near the end of the nineteenth century there were basically two traditions in American universities, all of which, for practical purposes, were private, non-profit institutions. The first, and unquestionably more important, of these traditions was that of the church-related college. These were schools founded either to promote religion and inculcate certain values or to train students for the ministry. And, of course, some schools did both. In one fashion or another the great bulk of private universities in America, ranging all the way from the very early schools like Harvard and Dartmouth to the later group of small midwestern colleges like Antioch or the primeval University of Chicago, had strong denominational influence.

The fact that many of these schools were founded in order to give religious training had a direct effect on the behavior of everyone concerned with these schools. Unlike the modern university, with many and diverse goals, these schools had a specific objective. The trustees, administrators, and faculty, as well as students, all understood that the school was basically a means to achieve doctrinal conviction. It could be said that the donors of funds were purchasing primarily religious training and only incidentally other kinds of education.

The founders of these schools, in effect, "purchased" their own utility in the form of religious training for their and others' children. Presumably their satisfaction came from the knowledge of the religious values held by the students. Had the market provided purveyors of college religious training, the founders of these schools might as well have taken advantage of market specialization and allowed others to produce what they purchased. As it was, they had to produce this commodity for their own use. Their situation was analogous to that of mid-nineteenth-century farmers who mortgaged their lands in order to help finance railroads. The farmers did not do this to become investors in the railroad industry. Their motivation was rather to purchase transportation in order to get their commodities to market. Their concern, as illustrated by numerous nineteenth-century law cases on the subject of *ultra vires,* was with access to freight cars rather than with the profitability from the operation of the railroad.

Under this approach, discretion in the allocation of the college's resources was very limited. The responsibility of all individuals to maximize the religious training purchased with the given funds was well understood. Thus, the behavior of trustees and administrators was not unlike that of any businessman interested in producing at a specific and definite cost the largest amount of a specific commodity possible; and the trust form of organization was eminently suited to this outlook. It allowed the donors of funds or the friends of the organization to manage the operation without any interference from market competitors; that is, they did not want the flexibility and potential for change inherent in a business firm competing in a marketplace. That form of organization would only have been appropriate for entrepreneurs planning to profit from the sale of education to consumers of it.

Another special aspect of academic denominationalism played a role in the development of modern universities. Probably because of constitutional doubts on the issue, these schools were regularly extended exemptions from local taxation. Most nonprofit institutions that received this privilege in late eighteenth- and early nineteenth-century America were church-related, and the First Amendment's interdiction of laws "respecting a religious establishment" was thus easily converted into an indirect form of government subsidy to denominational colleges. Again the legal history of this phenomenon is not altogether clear, and there were nondenominational charitable institutions in America as well. But the fact remains, nonetheless, that quite early this form of government subsidy was well established for private schools. Clearly, it influenced many school's founders to adopt the nonprofit form of organization.

The second great tradition in American private education, while not inconsistent with the other, is distinguishable enough to be addressed separately. This was the notion of elitist, liberal education. In this tradition, education was viewed as a kind of luxury "consumption good," designed to train an affluent class of aristocrats or dilettantes in the humane arts. Undoubtedly, a number of the private colleges originally founded as denominational schools moved into this second category. At the present a great many of these have ceased to acknowledge any denominational interests whatever.

Strangely, however, the political economy of this kind of school was not fundamentally different from that of the denominational school. These institutions were, in the truest sense of the word, "class" establishments, and the class was unmistakably upper. It would have been very difficult in nineteenth-century America to find many people who could afford the luxury of three or four years of humane studies. This would be true even though tuition was free and other costs were subsidized, since few students would have the necessary educational background, a vast number would simply have no interest, and an even larger number would not be able to afford the sacrifice of four years without gainful employment.

But be that as it may, these institutions were in large measure consciously managed so as to preserve them as intellectual and social sanctuaries for America's version of an aristocracy. Again, the trustees of such schools had a clear purpose by which to test their every action. So long as administrators and faculty understood the purpose, there could be no question about the location of authority.

Manifestly, the ultimate locus of control rested with those individuals who financed the institutions. It is probably the case that individuals giving large sums to quasi-denominational or nondenominational private schools did so with the idea of benefiting their own social class and perhaps occasionally the "deserving poor." This class, of course, was not a European-type aristocracy. However, that made no difference, since the goals were fundamentally the same; i.e., to insulate their children from other social classes, to educate them in a rather luxurious fashion, and, finally, to inculcate in them the values of the system in which their families had prospered.

There were certain characteristics of these schools, of which Princeton, Northwestern, Vanderbilt, and Stanford could serve as prototypes, that followed from their purpose and mode of organization. The individuals who gave large sums of money to these schools either became the trustees of the schools or selected the trustees or had fairly close relations with them. That is, these individuals, like the churches and religious donors to denominational schools, were still primarily interested in producing a certain kind of education for a select group of individuals. They did not intend to be establishing anything like a business firm selling to the public, but incidentally operated on a not-for-profit basis. Since the money was really used to "purchase" a commodity, trustees kept a close watch on who were admitted as students, who taught courses, and indeed what was taught.

Certainly, no one in most of these schools would have thought of admitting blacks, or even whites who could not readily afford some financial drain, albeit subsidized. When members of minority religious groups were admitted, it was inevitably on a strict quota basis. Brilliance and scholarship were not the virtues most highly regarded for either students or teachers. Loyalty to the cultural or religious ideals of the institution must have been far more important than grades, publications, or inventions. This is not to say the trustees were necessarily opposed to the other qualities in teachers but, rather, that there was no reason to focus exclusively on intellectuality.

Further, there must have existed something approaching an implicit oath of loyalty to the ideals and attitudes the institution was established to preserve. Certainly the notion of academic freedom as a protection for teachers in their search for truth would not have been advanced in most nineteenth-century universities. This is not to say that scientists would not have been concerned to protect their objectivity and integrity, but science was not the kingpin of universities then.

Clearly, if universities were to function efficiently as the means by which donors "produced" attitudes for a certain set of students, it was necessary to avoid a competitive market situation. This could only be guaranteed if the education was offered at a "bargain" price; that is, below full cost. If schools began to cover all costs by tuition, students or their parents would have been converted into "consumers" and would have exercised normal market controls over competing sellers. Only by maintaining the form of a nonprofit institution subsidizing, as it were, the students who could take advantage of the program could the donors continue to control the substance of what was taught, who taught it, and to whom it was taught. Thus, there were no "consumers" who could be sovereign, since no school was established to "sell" its product on a competitive, businesslike basis.

This pattern, which probably predominated in the late nineteenth century, generated much of the popular image of universities. The college graduate had not only an education but a certain social status that others aspired to. But it was not a potential for high income resulting from education that gave him this status; on the contrary, this status was proof that he had "already arrived," socially and financially.

In passing, we might note what this pattern would probably dictate for the behavior of college administrators. Presidents would be selected by the trustees to carry out their bidding on all aspects of educational policy. There would be no other constituency to which college administrators would even think of answering.

Disapproval by the faculty or students of administrative actions could only influence the administrator if the actions were also disapproved of by the trustees.

All in all, then, there was a fairly neat package, in which university donors caused the kind of education they wanted for certain students to be produced and the entire institution was managed to that end. While there was no consumer sovereignty on the part of students or their parents, at least in the usual sense, there was likewise none of the problems we find in the modern university. The reason for problems today, as we shall see, is not that the organizational form adopted by founders of colleges was not appropriate then. It is, rather, that it is no longer appropriate to the changed attitudes about education.

New Influences

Probably the pattern just described could have gone on almost indefinitely. As vocational training became more desirable, and as larger numbers of people recognized that education was a good investment, proprietary schools of various sorts developed. At one time these probably predominated in the United States in such areas as medicine, law, dentistry, accounting, engineering, and other vocational areas. The story of the disappearance of those schools is an interesting chapter in itself, but not directly germane to the present paper. Typically, these schools declined because of governmentally imposed "standards," which, in fact, were political devices to curtail competition for existing professionals. But the big change in American higher education patterns came with the expansion of state university systems, particularly after the Morrill Acts of 1862 and 1890.

State universities probably illustrate nicely the thesis of Allen Wallis that government welfare programs are generally adopted only when the need alleged is already being adequately served in the private sphere. The economic point of this is that only those already purchasing the particular service receive 100% of the value of the government's contribution. Anyone who was not already purchasing the service must value it at less than its market price; thus, he benefits less by the government's largess than the actual market consumer. The chances are pretty good that research would show political pressure for state universities to have come from the economic class that already realized the value of higher education for its children. Like all welfare programs, this one, too, was undoubtedly alleged to be for the welfare of the poor; that is, for those who could not "afford" college education for their children. In fact, as is true even today, the allocation of public funds to students in the form of university education usually represents a reallocation of wealth from the relatively poor to the relatively more affluent.

There were significant educational effects that

flowed directly from the introduction on a large scale of political forces into the world of higher education. Though the children of wealthier parents gained the advantage of this subsidized education, it was also true that there ceased to be any guiding purpose for these institutions. Especially with the constitutional inhibitions on religious training, the goal of state-operated universities became a matter of considerable uncertainty. We know, of course, that the tradition of liberal arts education survived in considerable measure. More important, as schools came to be thought of as places where one learned a vocation, political pressures pushed schools toward the more "practical" programs, ones designed to help students earn a living. Even today, the tradition of humane letters and liberal arts is felt more strongly in the private universities than the public ones. No longer does the provider of funds, now the taxpayer, have much opportunity to exercise control over the educational program offered. So long as state universities do not interfere with the interests of the politicians responsible for channeling public funds into these ventures, things go smoothly. But if politically unpopular activities become too prevalent, the government must respond.

With the advent of the public university, a great deal of the support that had formerly gone for private universities disappeared. Competition for students became much more keen, as few parents could afford to forgo the implicit subsidy of the low-tuition state university.

And very important for the analysis to follow, the demand for teachers became much greater. Since the state universities could not politically or legally hold to a particular religious or cultural standard, instructors began to be selected from religious and socioeconomic groups which were not regularly considered previously. These individuals, of course, could not necessarily be expected to feel a loyalty to a different culture. Thus, the attitudes prevalent on campuses began to undergo a radical shift, if for no other reason than that they became neutral or positivist, rather than religiously oriented or culturally directed.

Other important influences on the modern university are strictly twentieth-century developments. First among these would be high personal income tax rates, with contributions to nonprofit universities or foundations deductible from gross income. This had the effect of lowering the "price" of charity, thus increasing the amount of utility "purchased" through charitable contributions. This increase in contributions might have generated more of the kind of control traditional donors exercised over universities, but, by and large, it was too late. No longer could a donor "purchase" anything but the satisfactions afforded by his contributions to education as directed by others. Only in rare instances and for very large sums could he impose his will on the object of his charity. This might not be true of the modern foundation, which, on occasion, may make very large contributions. By and large, however, the foundations have avoided giving any positive direction to universities, while they have certainly done almost nothing to counteract economic and political biases of most of them. In effect, then, both individual and foundation donations have probably tended merely to strengthen the pattern which has developed in universities for other reasons.

Recent years have also seen a tremendous increase in the amount of government-sponsored research, as well as government contributions to private universities for buildings, salaries, and tuition. And, finally, the advent of large-scale private consulting, particularly by the science faculties, has probably had a significant influence on the behavior of academics.

The effect of most of these new influences has tended in the same direction. Trustees and other individual sources of funds who might have tried to direct the policies or values of universities are simply not as important to administrators and faculties as they originally were. As competition has driven the real income of faculties higher, the faculties have also discovered that a nonprofit institution allows them to take part of their gain in various nontaxable forms, like more leisure or time for research on a personally preferred topic. Furthermore, as government and foundations increased in financial importance relative to individual donors—at least for many of the specific things that individual faculty members wanted—it became more and more difficult for trustees to influence faculties at all. And as outside consulting and research became readily available for academics, this, too, tended to loosen the financial hold of donors and trustees.

There is no longer any way for trustees to keep faculty members "in line." There is not even a "line" for trustees, as such, at all. Their interest in serving has become only the quite weak reed of community status or prestige. Instead of being directed by trustees, the modern private university has become "democratized," with an almost total loss of trustee control over student admissions, faculty hiring, and curriculum.

Behavior of University Functionaries

The Trustees

The most significant characteristic of the modern university trustee is his almost total lack of real interest in exercising any authority. He could hardly feel a real personal responsibility for the "values of western civilization" or whatever amorphous goal he might talk about at annual dinners. He does not have any feeling, certainly, for the question of who, generally, should be admitted to receive the school's subsidy in the form of lower-than-full-cost tuition. This right was given up long ago, as American society culturally forbade the older, restrictive standards and as the faculty, the only group with a real interest in selecting the students, took over the task.

Somewhat similarly, the trustees have no power whatever to determine what views will be taught in universities. There are still denominational schools where this is not completely true, but, save these, the modern notion of "academic freedom" has given the faculty effective power over subject matter in the university and its curriculum. Particularly in very technical fields, this was said to have represented merely the trustees' deferring to the expertise of the faculty. But what that indicates is that the trustees had nothing significant to gain by exercising this power; therefore, it was no great loss to give it up to teachers who did have something to gain by it, as we shall see.

While it might be possible for one very wealthy individual to organize a university along certain lines, it would be extremely difficult for anyone to influence an existing institution by the use of donations. First of all, professional associations of teachers and accrediting agencies have removed some of the power to deal with that group. Secondly, laws now exist that forbid certain types of discrimination in the selection of students and faculty. Finally, even a very large donation to an existing institution does not give the donor any legal power of disposition over preexisting funds.

There is always a board of trustees that operates as a self-perpetuating oligarchy. Even though an individual may "buy" his way onto such a board, he will still be only one among many. This is not to say that in some instances wealthy individuals have not exercised considerable influence over an entire board of trustees, which in turn actually gave some direction to the university. Normally, however, this would require a rather unusual set of circumstances, including a top administrator committed to the goals of this individual.

Any prestige left to the position of university trustee no longer comes from the power the position carries. No longer are these favors that can be allocated to one's friends. Such prestige as there is today comes only from the traditional prestige of the office and certainly not from fighting for any particular ideology or standard. Although the trustees are still expected to assist in fund-raising for the university, it is largely on the same basis as they would assist in fund-raising for the local art gallery, orchestra, or museum. It is just that the university is usually larger and still carries greater prestige than other community activities. But it is doubtful whether, in years to come, the relative status position of universities' trustees will be much higher than that of any other comparable-sized eleemosynary institutions' trustees.

The last sporadic fights for the vestiges of control left in the hands of trustees are now being waged. These fights may frequently result in great losses of time, in embarrassment, or in unfavorable publicity for members of boards of trustees. These have become new "costs" of being a trustee. Consequently, we should anticipate that, in future years, there will be some lessened willingness on the part of prominent individuals to assume the risk of serving on a university board. Thus, trustees' power will shrink even more.

This is a rather bleak forecast for the future of boards of trustees of universities; in fact, that group seems well on its way to complete impotence. Since universities and faculties have developed independent sources of funds, there is not the compulsion that used to exist to appoint affluent trustees. In fact, the composition of these boards is already changing, as we find students, teachers, and even employees serving on the boards. It must be acknowledged, however, that for most schools there is still some concern with the flow of funds from trustees and their friends. Where that factor is still important, the college board tends to exercise more control of university policy. Probably this degree of control will never completely disappear.

The legal form of trustee "ownership" of the university is a fairly efficient one, and it has the added advantage of familiarity. Like the English monarchy, it would probably change only if the trustees actually tried again really to control academic policy. And that does not seem very likely, since there is really very little for them to gain by the exercise of such power. All indications are that the sterilization of boards of trustees will continue, with occasional signs of life here and there, usually based on an unusually strong individual personality. But these will be like comets that flash brilliantly for a while and then disappear.

The Administration

When we refer to the administration, we generally mean the top administrative executive, here called the president. Not surprisingly, the general style and character of a university president will reflect the real power interests within the institution. That is, he will be selected on the basis of characteristics that please those individuals actually exercising the selection power.

It should be possible, therefore, to make some accurate deductions about the characteristics that will be demanded under different selection-power arrangements. Thus, in the goal-directed, traditional universities, presidents were probably subservient to an active and powerful board of trustees. We would not expect such individuals to be selected for, or show, qualities of imagination, competitiveness, and innovation. Only as trustees delegated part of their managerial power to the president do we find imposing figures like William Murray Butler at Columbia or William Rainey Harper at Chicago. Unquestionably, such appointments reflected a true dedication on the part of trustees to creating an institution of very high academic standing.

But the much more significant change in preferred characteristics of college presidents came as the real decision-making power shifted from the trustees to the faculty. Whereas, in an earlier era, the trustees may have wanted simply a supply-and-personnel manager, the interest of faculties was in a different kind of president. Perhaps first and foremost they were interested in a fund-raiser. He was not supposed to bring his personal influence to bear on issues of educational policy. He was simply supposed to keep the money flowing in from outside sources.

Thus, as the main source of funds began to shift from individuals to large foundations and government, the interest of presidential selection committees shifted to individuals with political know-how or good contacts in the government and foundation worlds. Recently, as money matters have seemed to take a back seat to the explosive issue of campus violence, the search has been for men best suited for resolving disputes and mediating between contending factions. Thus, it is no accident that Duke, Case Western, and Harvard have in the past year tapped the deans of their law schools as top university administrators. But this is probably only temporary. As the violence dies down, faculties will again recognize that the president is the key man for raising funds, and probably the earlier presidential recruiting pattern will reappear.

None of this is to suggest that in some simpleminded fashion the committee of trustees that used to select presidents is now a committee of tenured professors. As we shall see, the traditional form in universities has been maintained, while the real power has shifted. In the case of presidential selection, it is largely a matter of the trustees having no interests that they feel need to be protected or furthered by the selection of an individual dedicated to those interests. The faculty, on the other hand, address themselves to amorphous but generally accepted standards like "a man of high academic reputation" or "someone prominent in the university world" to guarantee that the man selected is, in fact, dedicated to the kind of university that faculties want.

University presidents today have almost no authorized discretionary power over academic matters like faculty selection and course content. They can, however, still wield some influence by tactical use of their power over budget matters. A strong president, with trustee support, can use the budget as a lever to gain some academic policy ends. But actually, in crucial areas like personnel selection and course content, few presidents really have any preferences contrary to those of the faculties.

A skilled president can still make matters uncomfortable for professors who are personally obnoxious to him, but even that power must be used sparingly, since faculties today understand the techniques necessary to force a president to resign. If enough trustees are made uncomfortable or embarrassed by complaints rightly or wrongly aired by the faculty about the president, most trustees will probably take the easy way out. Since trustees usually have no great interest in the doctrinal aspects of the dispute between the president and the faculty, their best strategy is generally to capitulate in a face-saving way to the faculty. In the last few years we have seen numerous examples of precisely this process. Cornell is probably the most notable.

All of this is not to say that a university president is a eunuch simply there to do the faculty's bidding. The principal point is that it requires a very different personality to serve a goal-directed board of trustees than it does to serve an amorphous, ill-directed power group like a university faculty. But it is the latter that most presidents must serve today in order to survive.

The publicity given to university disruptions in recent years generally suggested that there was a power struggle going on, with the faculty and students on one side arrayed against the administration on the other. The trustees were normally depicted as sitting on the sidelines or else grudgingly intervening only when the situation had become hopeless. But that is not what the real struggle was. What we have been witnessing is simply one of the last battles in the conflict between faculties and trustees for control of universities. The ultimate conclusion to this struggle is already foregone, and these are mainly mopping-up operations by the faculties. The students' interest, apart from the fact that they were largely manipulated by the faculties, seems to have been mainly in having a good time.

In this struggle the administration frequently served as a scapegoat, though just as often it operated as a shield or a battering ram for the faculty in dealing with the trustees. Only in the few unusual cases of presidents with strong views and a strong personality was the president a significant force in this power struggle. Not unexpectedly, then, he felt an obligation to protect the power position of the trustees and, indeed, to protect the integrity of the trustees themselves. But, unless the board itself is highly unusual, the faculty need only bide its time until it can select a president who will behave as it wishes.

The Faculty

So much has been said about the economics of faculty behavior that very little that is new can be added here. Professors Rogge and Alchian have both pointed out many of the circumstances that flow from less-than-full-cost tuition, and James Buchanan has shown how the university provides insulation between the economic force of the buyers (students) and the producers (faculty) so that no normal market response to demand is likely. It is, indeed, a topsy-turvy world in which grown men actually receive great powers with no responsibility for how they are wielded and large rewards without having to produce anything in return.

As we saw earlier, the development of American universities can be viewed as a transition from an arrangement in which trustees or donors, in effect, purchased an economic good to one in which we think of students as purchasers of a different economic good. The trustees established certain arrangements for the allocation of the educational goods it was in their power to distribute. The thing that has now changed so radically is the trustees' ability to secure any personal satisfaction or gain from the power to allocate this good. Since they could no longer guarantee that the kind of education they were offering certain students would be accepted by the students, they had less incentive to "buy" this right. But the power to make this allocation did not disappear as a result of the trustees' loss of interest in allocating in a particular way. Faculties developed real interests in exercising this power, and it was a simple matter for the faculty to move into the power vacuum created by the trustees' loss of interest, since no one else offered any objective standards for selection of students.

It was, of course, very much in the interest of faculties to select the most intelligent and intellectual students they could for admission to the university. There were many reasons for this. In the first place, these students were simply more enjoyable to teach. Related to this is the fact that outside sources of funds are always more available to a school that has a "good reputation." Since academic reputation came to be based on the quality of students, a strong incentive was built into the system to secure as good students as possible, since this, in turn, meant a greater claim on public or private funds.

In a slightly different vein, the faculty preferred
intellectual students to make their own work easier.
Frequently, this simply meant that inexpensive or free
research assistance was readily available to the teacher.
Related, but probably more important, was the fact
that better students frequently became teachers; they
could thus carry their own professors' fame with them.
This last point, of course, is more relevant for graduate
students than undergraduates, but was all part of the
intellectualization of universities.

There is another reason, too, why this demand for
intelligent students developed. As faculties ceased to
be selected on the basis of commitment to either religious or cultural ideals, some other objective standards
for discriminating between those to be hired and those
who were not to be hired were necessary. Camaraderie,
similarity of outlook, friendships all play a role in this,
but they cannot be the announced and avowed criteria
for selection. Only one possible criterion suggests itself, that of intelligence and scholarly accomplishment.
The race for senior professorships became, in effect, a
race to produce the most highly regarded scholarly
works. This, in turn, created a value system permeat-
ing the entire university. As Professor Tonsor has
pointed out, this may have very little to do with the
search for objective truth in most areas of scholarship,
but it did tend to put a premium on certain intellectual
characteristics, not the least of which were high IQ,
verbal facility, and an ability to copy and regurgitate

the works of others in the profession without seeming to plagiarize them. Quite clearly, if professors were to act as if they honestly believed in the standard of intellectualism, they must extend this to the selection of students as well. One wonders at times, however, how many would not have preferred to select only pretty girls if other constraints were not present.

In recent years we have witnessed a somewhat strange phenomenon. Faculties have insisted on the selection of black students for admission to college exclusively on the basis of color and regardless of their lack of the usual intellectual achievements. Part of the reason for this departure from direct self-interest may have been the money available from government and other sources for black-student programs. For the most part, however, the professors were simply following their own inclinations, since there seemed to be no cost to them in doing so. But it is interesting to notice what is now happening. The expansion of outside funds has stopped, and there have actually been cutbacks. Those individuals who wished to establish desirable positions for themselves have already done so, and the rest find that they receive little satisfaction any longer from the issue. Furthermore, the black students who are ill-equipped for the work they confront demand a great deal more time and effort than the faculties originally contemplated. Interest is clearly beginning to wane in special programs for black students, and the next few years will probably witness, under various rationalizations, a return to the standard of scholastic ability as the near-exclusive criterion for admission, other than payment of tuition. The cost of this episode will be a small generation of very peculiarly educated black students convinced of the hypocrisy of a white university world that did not live up to its promises.

There is one other odd aspect to the policy decision that has been made to allocate the available educational subsidy to the more intelligent. Since local and federal taxes underwrite the cost of education to a significant degree, the universities are involved in a peculiar reallocation of wealth, in this case from the relatively less intelligent to the relatively more intelligent. That this is probably undesirable public policy goes without saying, but the rationalizations and dogma of intellectualism run very deep.

Although the change in desired characteristics for students has been one of the most significant results of the shift in authority from trustees to faculty, other aspects of the shift have been written about more frequently. Probably no other has received quite the attention given to the professors' singleminded interest in not teaching. The light teaching load has become almost the stock joke among university faculties today. And, of course, the principal device for attracting a "star" has long been the promise of little or no teaching. Undoubtedly, this reflects to a considerable extent the greater payoff to professors from research and consulting, but the significant thing is that there is no meaningful way of rewarding a professor for more or better teaching, and thus competing for the time he spends on other pursuits. This, of course, was not the case when trustees took responsibility for running universities; it is, rather, one of the direct results of the shift to faculty power. Only if someone has a direct interest, financial or other, in transmitting knowledge to students will there be any increase in the incentive to each. At this time, the incentives are very small, if not actually negative.

The same idea runs throughout other administrative policies in faculty-run institutions. The faculties argue that these matters are not really their responsibility, since they do not exercise universitywide authority. That is true. But it is also true that the aspects of university life that most affect students educationally come through the academic departments, and here the faculties reign supreme. We find, for instance, that the list of courses offered in a department will strongly reflect the individual, and often very peculiar, interests of the faculty and not, in any degree, the interests of the students. Graduate students will naturally be preferred to undergradates, and gradually budgets and programs will be shaped to that end. The policy of the department and the university must be very liberal with regard to leaves of absence and consulting. And, of course, the faculty must not be asked to spend much time out of class with undergraduates. Signs on faculty doors like "Office hours—Wednesday, 2–3 P.M." are

not uncommon. They are outdone only by signs reading "Office hours—by appointment only."

Another more serious consequence of faculty control
of universities develops in the area of faculty hiring.
Again we can draw on some of the economic behavioral theories of Armen Alchian to set the general
framework for this discussion. Basically, faculty members making decisions about hiring colleagues are subject to almost no competitive market constraints. Like
the public utility manager who cannot take home all
the earnings he might be able to produce for the company, the faculty, too, tries to maximize its self-interest
at the office. As a result, tenure faculty will inevitably
look for young professors who (a) will not disrupt the
department and (b) have views that seem reasonable
to the senior people. Given the proclivity for personality fights sometimes to follow doctrinal lines, these
two may not even be very different, but, in any event
for present purposes, the second is the more interesting.

The problem for tenure professors considering a new
man is to find out what his real views are. By and large,
fairly safe guesses can be made. Actually, little attention is paid to other than the appearance, the personality, and perhaps the level of intellect of a candidate
for a teaching position. Much more important is the
recommendation given him by a senior professor under
whom he has done his doctoral research. Since the
views of that individual will almost certainly be widely
known, it can be safely assumed that any graduate

student he strongly recommends will have substantially the same point of view. Graduate students who understand this process ingratiate themselves with their senior professors by never advancing views fundamentally contrary to those of the older man.

This process almost guarantees a kind of monolithic uniformity of viewpoints, at least in those academic areas where complete objectivity is not possible (and perhaps even in the hard sciences where this objectivity is claimed). An open market for varying points of view would mean that varying views would be publicized and schools selected by students on the basis of their preference. At any given moment, the professors already in teaching have little incentive to create this kind of competition. It would, of course, almost automatically result if schools were generally profit-oriented, competitive firms. It should be noted that there are some exceptions to the generalization about monolithic viewpoints. An economics department like that of the University of Chicago or the political science department at the University of Rochester does attract students because of the publicized point of view of these departments, but such "sports" are rare.

Since a professor competes for a higher salary from universities rather than for a higher payment from students, faculty members tend to write for the former audience and to hold views that will not cause them to lose professional status. This further reinforces the pressures for a single point of view to be popular at any given moment in all departments in all universities within a given discipline. Change in this general viewpoint can come only very slowly, much in the style of changes in taste in the arts. Thus, if even a radical point of view becomes popular in a field, then, regardless of its merits and its lack of popularity in the world at large, it becomes nearly impossible to root it out or even to challenge it from within the university. Almost every area of the social sciences and humanities reflects the process just described.

The Students

The role of graduate students has been sufficiently explored in connection with the question of faculty appointments. But the position of undergraduates still deserves some additional consideration. Though the more vocal of these students may talk about the "reactionary" trustees and the "fascist" administration, the real truth is that among the various participants in the university community, the only real and significant conflict of interest exists between the faculty and the undergraduate students. Each of these groups wants more of exactly the same thing, and that is the faculty's time. Students want smaller classes, more courses, more liberal faculty office hours, and more individual conferences. The faculties avoid these things as much as they can and "jokingly" say how nice the university would be if there were no students.

As has been well described, particularly by James Buchanan, there is really no way that students can make their demands felt in this nonprofit environment. Those who make decisions in universities cannot profit personally by operating the university in the educational interests of students. The result, therefore, is from the students' point of view an appalling disregard of their wishes. A lot of what passes as modern permissiveness at the university level would more accurately be characterized as utter disinterest. Today this is being reflected in such matters as parietal rules, grading policy, so-called bulletin board courses, no attendance requirements, pass-fail grading, and many other devices passed off as innovations.

There are two principal factors that have prevented students from more effectively revolting against this monolithic system. One, obviously, was the draft, but the repeal of the college students' exemption removed that circumstance. The other is much more complicated. In many occupations, there is simply no way to secure the necessary government licensing without showing compliance with certain educational prerequisites. This is true of such popular fields as medicine, law, teaching, architecture, and many others. Obviously, many students do not realize why they are in a lockstep from high school to college to a professional school, and they probably see this simply as an initiation rite that our culture requires of its young. That they do not particularly care for it is clear from the variety of suggestions students make for varying their educational fare. Unfortunately, the one appropriate suggestion, forcing universities to compete for the students' favor, is unthinkable to them, since they have been so carefully taught through high school and college that that form of competition is evil and immoral.

The Alternatives Considered

Basically, there are three organizational schemes for the operation of universities. These are the free-market organization, dictatorship, and a cooperative system. The university world is presently in the process of passing from the second to the third of these without the first ever having been seriously tried. Consumer preference could operate in this field as well as in any other, and meaningful competition with no significant external costs could prevail. The means for reaching such a state of affairs are simple to describe, but politically they are very unlikely to occur.

First of all, the government would have to get out of the education business itself. No really strong argument has ever been made for government ownership and operation of universities. As at least a step in that direction, the state should give students tuition chits for use in any university of their choice. This step alone could make a tremendous difference in the quality of higher education offered.

Next, both state and federal tax exemptions for not-for-profit universities should be repealed, as should the deduction for federal income tax purposes of contributions to universities. These are nothing more than indirect subsidies by government to private educational institutions, and there is no apparent justification for this reallocation of taxpayers' wealth.

If these tax changes were made and other direct subsidies were cut off, the only "free" source of funds for private universities would be income from their existing endowments. There would also be tremendous legal difficulties in ever converting the use of the trust funds from a nonprofit to a proprietary end. In fact, however, if the de facto ownership of the faculty were recognized by giving them shares of stock or other transferable share interests in the university, there would be less outcry about the conversion. Actually, the identity of the owners of a proprietary university would be less important than the fact that transferable interests existed. This would, in time, guarantee some of the competitive benefits realized by corporations from the fact that ownership interests are transferable.

In any event, as all subsidies disappeared, universities would find it in their interest to behave more like proprietary institutions. They would, at least, have to cover all real costs by the income from their endowment and operations. Clearly, when that occurred, proprietary institutions could effectively compete and in all likelihood demonstrate that they answer market demands better than nonprofit institutions. It's a nice dream!

The second model for a university is fundamentally the one described as the nineteenth-century norm earlier in this paper. While it utilizes the nonprofit organizational scheme, it still bears a number of market earmarks. Perhaps it is most appropriate to look at the founders and supporters of nineteenth-century colleges as buyers of education for others, not sellers to the students. The relevant payoff in that system was not measured in terms of the value of the education to the students. Rather, it was measured in terms only of the utility to the trustees or donors. These two values, as is true generally in the economics of charity, may be quite different. Today we tend to look at education as the commodity being sold, and we tend to talk about the students as consumers. Consequently, we can only measure the utility of the present system in terms of the value of the education to the students.

It is arguable that the great problems in university education today stem from a failure to recognize the conversion from a market for satisfying the demands of financial donors ("purchasers" of charitable satisfaction) to a market for meeting the educational demands of students. The nonprofit organizational arrangement was adopted in the earlier period when that was appropriate to the goals of the donors. But as the nature of the market began to change, that organizational scheme became an anachronism. It is not surprising that the real locus of power shifted, since the original wielders of power, the trustees, no longer had any real interest in it. We have willy-nilly fallen into an organizational system for the marketing of education that is almost totally inappropriate to answer the demand of the real consumer today.

The third model, the one rapidly becoming the only one in the university world, is the co-op model. This term is meant to imply joint ownership and management by a large group of people. It does not mean that there are no property rights in university assets. On the contrary, it is quite clear that faculty has managed to establish a strong claim to being considered "owners" of the modern university. But multiple ownership without delegated centralized management guarantees results quite different from those found in a typical business corporation.

Because faculty members eschew market allocations of resources and prefer the model of political systems, the tendency in universities today is toward a form of democratic decision-making. In its most extreme form, at schools like Columbia and Cornell, this takes the form of a constituent assembly. This is a legislative body with representation by faculty, students, and the administration. But, as in Orwell's *Animal Farm,* some of these are more equal than others; clearly, the faculty represents the only continuing identifiable group with specific interests in the way universities are operated. Student representatives come and go, and there is no logical reason why student solidarity should even exist, much less present a permanent base for student political interests. The administration, as we have already seen, tends simply to reflect the interests of whichever constituency happens to be more powerful, so it is clear that the administration will generally support the wishes of the faculty. The trustees, by and large, will not expend great energies or resources in fighting for views and outcomes that cannot make much difference to them.

The net result of this form of administration and decision-making is inevitably a negotiated compromise of the various conflicting interests within the faculty. Various parts of the faculty, unlike the administration and the students, will actively fight for a large part of the pie. But overt fights would weaken the faculty vis-à-vis the other groups. Therefore, to avoid this, various power groups within the faculty will negotiate and bargain until they have established their claims.

It will, then, be in everyone's interest to prevent disruptions. In effect, each contending interest group gives up any responsibility for overall university affairs in exchange for the right to be financed and then left alone. The function of the administration and the trustees in this model will be to insure that sufficient funds flow in, either from government or private sources, to allow everyone to survive in his present state.

It might be noticed—and not occasion surprise—that this is fundamentally the model we find in European universities today. It is consistent with the legal theory in civil-law countries that universities are independent, quasi-sovereign powers. They are permanently funded by government; there is very little innovation or change; each department or institute becomes highly bureaucratized; advancement in the system is exclusively through personal favor rather than ability; there is little flexibility or adaption to change; and the students understand that they are receiving a very poor education.

One of the less-publicized effects of this developing organizational system is the extreme difficulty in implementing any innovation or change. Since any new idea is potentially destabilizing, everyone presently satisfied with his condition opposes any change. This is especially so if the innovator suggests that existing departments or individuals give up any resources in order to finance a new program. Consequently, any new program must be funded by entirely new funds, which will be given expressly for that purpose and not to the university at large. This probably explains the large number of so-called institutes in European schools and the increasing number in America. It becomes nearly impossible in this system for a university to react to changes in market demand or new circumstances without wild and disruptive fights.

This entire arrangement is bolstered by arguments about academic freedom, which is the American version of the pseudosovereignty enjoyed by European universities. In either case, it is most often a claim for power without responsibility.

One last implication of this arrangement might be noted. The people who survive and prosper in this system will tend to be those with the characteristics most adaptable to this environment. We have already seen that that means a low level of innovation and, by indirection, strong aversion to risk. There is no reason to believe that people with these characteristics will not reflect them in their doctrinal views. In other words, it would be highly surprising for a large population that has established its suitability for a bureaucratic, non-profit-oriented, political environment to advocate market solutions to any problem.

Thus, it may be that the university world today attracts people who inherently favor collectivist, statist, nonmarket attitudes. The entire university world then becomes a massive device, heavily financed by tax-payers, for propagating a point of view that, while perhaps not illogical for those espousing it, excludes the fair consideration of any other doctrine. The real costs of having nonprofit educational institutions may, in this sense, be vastly greater than we have generally recognized.

Essay Four

Authority, Power, and the University

Stephen J. Tonsor

Stephen J. Tonsor was educated at Blackburn College, Carlinville, Illinois; the University of Zürich; the University of Munich; and was awarded a Ph.D. in history by the University of Illinois in 1955. He also holds an LL.D. from Blackburn College. He has taught in the fields of European history of ideas and historiography at the University of Michigan since 1954. In 1961 he was awarded the Class of 1923 prize for distinguished teaching. He has lectured and published widely on American education and public policy formation. He is currently a North Central Association Associate, Associate Editor of Modern Age, *a member of the Mont Pelerin Society, and Adjunct Scholar at the American Enterprise Institute. He has served on the Executive Council of the Catholic Historical Association, as President of the Philadelphia Society, and as the secretary of a foundation. Dr. Tonsor is currently completing a book on the pre-Hitlerite German Youth movement. During the year 1972–73 he was visiting research fellow at the Hoover Institution at Stanford University, Palo Alto, California.*

M en have always been puzzeld by both power and authority. The source of either is mysterious and the uses of either unclear. They are quite commonly confused so that men and institutions who attempt to convert authority into power discover that spiritual realities cannot be defined in terms of Newtonian mechanics, and those who seek to translate power into authority learn that no human undertaking is so difficult as the legitimation of coercion.

In recent times, no one has said of either a university president or an educational institution as St. Matthew said of Jesus, "For he taught them as one having authority, and not as the scribes." John Searl, former vice-chancellor for student affairs of the University of California at Berkeley, has remarked that "the unreality of the new left is its most touching quality." Only the new left could seriously propose that the university campus was a great power center whose capture by the new left would enable it to revolutionize that parent society. The fact is clear and unmistakable that in 1971 the university possesses neither authority nor power. It is equally clear that it can have no power in our society until it regains its authority and that the power which it will then be able to exert will have no relationship to the power which Chairman Mao asserts grows out of the barrel of a gun.

It is clear, then, that the authority which the university possesses is a social authority freely given by the whole of society, just as the support and financing of the university is, in the final analysis, social. The university cannot, consequently, exercise its authority or sustain itself if it loses sight of the wholeness of society and places its resources at the command of a financial or cultural elite or permits itself to be exploited and victimized by a deviant minority group bent upon aggrandizement and tyranny. As soon as it becomes apparent in any society that those things which in some sense are the property of all are in the possession and use of the few, no matter how fine their morals and how noble their characters, the society renounces its allegiance and withdraws its support. Moreover, the very exercise of proctorship by the self-selected elite in such a situation is vastly corrupting and personally corrosive. Those who, above all others, should persuade through reasoned discourse are tempted to apologize, to lie, and to coerce.

The university does not belong to the students; it

does not belong to the faculty; it does not belong to any special pressure group in the society that happens to feel the call to revolution or a prophetic mission. The university belongs to the whole of the society or the corporate reality which brought it into existence and which sustains it. Every administrator who capitulates before a "nonnegotiable demand" sacrifices the authority of his institution to the power of a minority. However, not only does he "deauthorize" the institution, making it impossible for the college or university to educate, but he cuts off his institution from the support and the goodwill of the society as a whole.

Preemption and Occupation

The destructive influences of minority groups of students and social activists in subverting and corrupting the educational ideals and processes of the colleges and universities are well known. Less well known, but no less destructive of the institutional authority of the university, is the fashion in which certain views and schools of thought preempt and occupy all the positions available within departments and even within whole disciplines. In the fields of the humanities and social sciences there is hardly a proposition which goes beyond the restatement of primitive folk-truth which is not the subject of widespread and informed debate, which in every instance calls into question the very basis in reality of the opposed parties' vision of the truth. In the social sciences and the humanities there is no Truth but only partial truths, while in the natural sciences Sir Karl Popper has taught us to mistrust any generalization which does not suggest a maximum of experiments aimed at its destruction. How odd, then, that whole disciplines have fallen under the sway of unprovable hypotheses and undemonstrated theorems.

In these great matters, which concern man and his society, the humanist and the social scientist carry over into their science the overt and even unconscious commitments of their daily lives. The point from which one starts does make a difference. Religious commitment or a lack of it does make a difference in philosophy; a specific political commitment does make a difference in the theory of the political scientist; a particular view of man's nature does make a difference in the work of the critic and the vision of a poet.

In the fall of 1969, the Carnegie Commission on Higher Education took a survey sample of 60,447 faculty members in American universities. These faculty members were asked to characterize themselves politically "at the present time." In the discipline of sociology, for example, 80.8 percent of the professors surveyed identified themselves as liberals or leftists. One tenth of one percent identified themselves as "strongly conservative." How, one is compelled to ask, is debate on fundamental social issues possible when there is such overwhelming uniformity of political and theoretical social commitment? Sociology is not an anomaly. Most of the "social sciences" and the humanities show a distribution not remarkably different.

In many colleges and universities the field of the study of religion is totally excluded. Universities with professors whose specialty is the religion of Tibet do not have a single professor who specializes in Judaism or Christianity. It may be true that religion is one of the most pervasive and fundamental of man's activities, but this fact is simply unrecognized by many colleges and universities. The fashionable agnosticism and atheism of most faculty members ought to be of concern to college administrators. That those whose vocation is the exploration, understanding, transmission, and criticism of ideas in a society should be alienated from and hostile to its formative influence should be a matter for anxiety. It is customary, of course, to argue that such questions are inconsequential to the discovery of truth and effective education; and yet we would be justified in expressing concern were a scientist to assert that he was convinced that nature was chaotic and that there was no possibility, even in terms of probability, of anticipating regularity.

University Discrimination

Finally, the community at large distrusts university faculties because they are so homogenous in terms of religion, race, and sex. For the first time, Negroes are finding on faculties an acknowledgment that the experience of being Negro does make a difference in the way one perceives the subject matter of the social sciences and the humanities. To be black, for example, ought to sensitize one in a special way to the economic costs of prejudice and the social costs of lawlessness. To be black ought to sensitize one in a special way to the promise of American institutions and ought to instill in one an intense dedication to the success of American ideals. I anticipate that in the long run the impact of Negro scholarship and Negro perceptions on the intellectual life of the university cannot constitute anything but an enrichment. That enrichment cannot, however, take place if the Negro scholar withdraws into his own course and segregates himself from the conflict of ideas and the noise of debate which should characterize every university campus.

What the Negro is on the point of achieving is still denied both to women and to Roman Catholics. To be sure, there is token representation of both groups on most faculties, especially those of state universities, but neither group has been permitted to make its full contribution to the life and scholarship of contemporary society. We are all acquainted with the role which nineteenth-century liberalism played in dispelling the clouds of prejudice which surrounded both women and Catholics, but we need now to reassert those principles with respect to university teaching.

The university cannot, and ought not to, speak with one voice on any subject. Professors and students ought not to involve their institutions in the controversies of the society. Those compulsive newspaper advertisements in which intellectuals proclaim their support of the current orthodoxies and to which they are careful always to append their institutional identification remind one of nothing so much as the patent medicine recommendations which once filled working-class and farm weeklies. Medical faculties ought not to speak on the subject of harvesting grapes, microbiologists on the subject of Soviet-American relations, sociologists on the subject of theology. It is a sobering truth that most contemporary intellectuals cannot distinguish an opinion from a fact. They are convinced that thinking makes it so, and they employ the Ph.D. in the way in which Southern sheriffs of a decade ago were said to have employed electrical cattle prods. How pleasant it would be to hear even one professor say when pressed by a television interviewer in the course of a discussion of a controversial topic, "I don't know." I cannot recall a single instance of that sort.

The Primary Commitment

Lastly, the public authority of the university is dependent upon its commitment to research and education rather than a general willingness to perform any task anyone or any group in society at large imposes on it. The university is not a general-purpose social institution. It is not suited to the solution of social problems, the amelioration of misery and misfortune, the reformation of character, or the transformation of culture. To be sure, the university produces skills and knowledge which will achieve all these ends, but it does not and cannot directly perform any of them. When a university gets into the building of low-rent housing, and that not even for students, as is the case at Stanford, the university is quite simply disloyal to its primary commitment. Some students at the University of Michigan are now demanding that the university provide "free" health care to all the children of the community in which the university is located. It could do so only by neglecting its fundamental commitment. The university is not engaged in the cure of souls; it is not engaged in organizing for political and social revolution; it is not in the business of providing necessary social or health services. Sometimes specific services are a by-product of the teaching and research function of the university, but they are never to be thought of as a part of its mission.

In his Godkin Lectures at Harvard in 1963, one year before the advent of the "free speech" movement at Berkeley, Clark Kerr noted that, "The university is so many things to so many different people, that it must, of necessity, be partially at war with itself." But not only is it at war with itself, it is at war with important segments of its society. The demands which it seeks to meet are not reconcilable and the conflicting roles which it seeks to play are not compatible. There cannot be a restoration of the authority of the university until the university returns to its primary role as teacher. To be sure, the maintenance and criticism of the cultural tradition, the development and preservation of method and research in the pursuit of new knowledge are all important ancillary activities, but they are ancillary and must always be subordinated to the teaching function and the research performed must be open and freely discussable.

Research institutes and research professors whose essential commitment falls outside the realm of teaching should not be associated with the university. Both are terribly important in our society, but both bring pressures to bear on the structure of university education which will, in the not so very long run, destroy it.

It is quite possible that the state universities, due to a tradition which goes all the way back to the Northwest Ordinance and which found its most typical expression in the Morrill Act, will find it impossible to break the ties to service and research which the state thrusts upon them. If that, indeed, is the case, we have been provided with yet another argument for taking the state out of the business of educating altogether.

Technicians of Adjustment

Even were the university to eschew all the tasks and beguilements thrust upon it by society and decide to live in uncorrupted innocence and poverty, it is unlikely that it would regain its authority in society so long as it refuses to exercise such authority as it still possesses. So long as university administrations are not the masters in their own house, they are ill-equipped to exert any degree of mastery in the world outside. At the present time, typical university presidents are the amoeba-like victims of every aggressive group on campus. Their powers of ingestion and cooperation have been enormous, and such success as they have had in keeping the universities functioning, even at a minimal level, has followed from the fact that they have, to date, been able to meet virtually every demand, no matter how outrageous, with a concession. They have not been educational statesmen—not even educational bureaucrats—rather, they have been technicians of adjustment.

In many instances the current style of university administrators has succumbed to violence and power because, anti-intellectual by nature, they distrusted the play of mind, the open debate, and the laborious process by which ideas are examined and tested. A number of them, such as Clark Kerr and Robben Fleming, derived their previous experience in the field of labor arbitration, where the essential problems are dealt with by adroitly balancing power rather than by protecting the consumer. Clark Kerr described this new style multiversity president aptly when he wrote: "The president in the multiversity is leader, educator, initiator, wielder of power; he is also officeholder, caretaker, inheritor, consensus seeker, persuader, bottleneck. But he is mostly a mediator."

If the university is to regain its lost authority in American society, it must find university administrators who see their mission in providing something more than, again as Clark Kerr so ably expressed it, "football for the alumni, parking for the faculty, and sex for the students." The university and college president must once more play the role of educational statesman. He must set the policy, establish the priorities, and create the conditions which will make it possible for his institution to accomplish its objective.

Above all, he must have a *clear vision of what the objective is.* The terrible sense of drift in American higher education must be dispelled. Institutions must regain some sense of their uniqueness and their purpose. Church-related colleges must refuse to undergo further secularization, the coeducational mania must be resisted by those few schools which still believe that the separation of the sexes makes educational sense, the liberal arts college must resist the temptation to turn itself into a diminutive state university, and those schools which pride themselves on a tradition of curricular experimentation or on religious or social homogeneity or diversity must continue their separate and unique ways. It is only, however, through the determined leadership of an individual or individuals indifferent to the homogenizing pressures of contemporary American society that this objective can be achieved.

Intransigent Faculty

Any college or university president who at the present moment determines to make his institution unique in mission, curriculum, instructional method, student body, or educational philosophy will discover very quickly that his great enemy is not the alumni or the board of trustees or even the student body, but his own faculty.

There are, to be sure, areas of college and university education in which the faculty is sovereign. They are not, however, those areas of sovereignty usually marked out by faculties. Very obviously, the faculty member either singly or as the member of a corporate body determines educational standards, has control over course content and conduct in the classroom, and is the final authority in matters of grades and certification. The faculty cannot and should not even attempt to legislate in matters of curriculum, conduct, budget, or institutional administration. Faculty meetings are neither political nor legislative bodies. In their present form they resemble nothing so much as a Polish parliament. At their best they should be consultative bodies in which the educational needs of the institution are discussed and in which administrative policy is implemented.

The Power to Decide

Only the administration together with the trustees can effectively set goals and determine policy. Trustees represent the whole corporate body of the institution. They constitute both its social and temporal dimension. They keep the institution true to itself and responsive to the society which it serves. Ultimately, all decisions in the institution are political decisions and the governing board is the only truly political body within the institution. It does, in fact, possess a constituency and exercises a legitimate power.

Although the governing board is the policymaking instrument within the institution and the ultimate source of power, it exercises its authority through the administration; and its policies, in the final analysis, are formulated by the administration. The administration consults with the faculty and formulates and carries out the will of the governing body.

It is obvious that the relationship between the administration and the governing board must be one of trust and confidence; but, while it is a truism, it must also be added that the confidence and trust which governing boards exhibit are not infrequently abused. After all, trustees and regents are active, busy men badgered and harassed by a multitude of demands. They have a short attention span, an even shorter memory, and they are ill-informed and, for the most part, ill-prepared to govern the institutions which they guide. I believe it is necessary, given the current condition of higher education, to provide governing boards with a secretary independent of the administration. The secretary to the governing board would be charged not with policy formation or day-to-day administration but, rather, with an investigative role. His task would entail the examination of administrative proposals, budgets, and appointments. He would provide the necessary extramural expertise which alone could insure that the decisions of the administration fall into line with the policy of the governing board. His investigative role would be especially important in budgetary and personnel matters.

The Student's Role

Since 1964 it has frequently been assumed that students should have a special role in university governance. Disciplinary matters have frequently been placed into the hands of student governments; and, increasingly, students have been given a role in the distinctive province of the faculty. Today at major universities students determine course offerings, decide on questions of accreditation and examination, pass on questions of academic discipline, and now seek to pass on appointments, salary increases, and tenure. A number of the elite colleges and universities have recently appointed student members to their governing bodies. Many of these concessions to the youth culture and the cult of relevance have been made in the genuine desire to make the university responsive to student needs. Where those needs are educational, students are remarkably ill-prepared to judge or to pass on policy.

The point of effective student control over education is the moment when the student chooses a college or university. His choice, of course, is never irrevocable; and he can always vote, as students have often voted, with his feet. Student governance beyond this point is unthinkable, and no self-respecting faculty member who is concerned for the integrity of his discipline and his right to teach will prostrate himself and his discipline before a student tyranny. It has, of course, been observed that student activists and the contemporary administrators are natural allies. Both love committee meetings, both place power above principle, and both are deeply anti-intellectual.

Finally, the administration must be given adequate freedom by the governing body to carry through the day-to-day policy decisions and operation of the institution. Governing bodies must establish, in consultation with the administration, policy and budget. They must check regularly to see that day-to-day policy and appointments are in keeping with the institutional objectives established by the governing board, but they must not attempt to perform the functions of the administration. The most important choice any governing board makes is in the appointment of a president. They should not be afraid to change their minds if the man they appoint is too little in harmony with policies of the governing board. At the present time, there seems to be a reluctance to fire a college president, even when he deliberately lies to the governing board.

The whole question of student discipline in matters both of academic and personal conduct is much disputed at the present time. Most of the elite universities and colleges have gone over to the notion that any conduct short of a felony is permissible on the part of either faculty or students, and if a court of law disciplines a student, further and other institutional discipline would represent "double jeopardy" and would be unfair, illegal, and inadmissible.

But at the same time the student claims an exemption from institutional standards, he claims an exemption from the laws and commonly held standards of his society. Administrators and students alike seem to envision the campus as an extraterritorial enclave where the rules of civility and the laws of the polity do not prevail. For nearly a decade, members of the so-called youth culture have been advising the young not to trust anyone over thirty, though the one abiding impression left with the public is that the young believe, or at least believed until recently, that no matter how outrageous their behavior the society at large would make excuses and would temper the wind to the shorn lambs. The idea that local police forces should be excluded from the campus, that felonies involving drug abuse and other campus criminal activities should not be punished in the courts, that violence should be tolerated as a form of legitimate protest, and that once a student has been arrested the legal resources of the institution should be made available to him all presuppose a separate and extralegal status for students which no sane society can countenance. If universities and colleges are to renew and maintain their status and authority in American life, the citizenry at large will need some assurance that there is, in fact, equal justice under the law and not preferential treatment for the college offender.

The Funding Problem

Every reform and every movement to return the colleges and universities to their essential function will fail unless it is accompanied by a systematic reform of the funding of higher education. The call for full-cost tuition is the single most important reform which it is possible to make in the field of education generally. It is especially important in higher education because nothing has so corrupted college and university education as what Robert Nisbet has called "the higher capitalism." The "higher capitalism" means that colleges and universities have sold out to foundations, government, and every group requesting research or service and capable of paying for it. The lure of money has been used for three decades to distract and divert institutions of higher education from their instructional mission. Professors are aware that the rewards lie in areas outside the classroom, and students know that professors no longer take teaching seriously.

Taxes, gifts, foundation grants, federal subsidies on a lavish scale, and contract research cannot pay the educational bill. If we are to reintroduce order in the house of intellect we must pass the costs of higher education to the only person who can and should pay the bill: the student.

When the student foots the bill, many of the present distortions in higher education will disappear. There will, in the first place, be some honesty in cost accounting, and undergraduate tuitions will not be used as they currently are at many major universities to subsidize an inordinately expensive program of graduate studies. Expensive innovations in instruction will show up immediately in increased tuition costs, and the "research professor" whose chief function is to lend intellectual distinction to his institution through his publication record will be a thing of the past. Professors will once more teach three 3-hour courses per semester, and students will find that professors are responsive to their needs and their requests. It may seem odd that enabling students to pay full-cost tuitions is a more likely way to give students an effective voice in their educations than placing them on governing boards.

Curriculum and instruction will once more be both responsive and relevant, and will provide the wide variety of training necessary both to the individual and the society. It is absurd to believe that once the source of income has shifted from government and the foundations to the student, the "vice presidents for development" and the legislative coordinators will not soon find themselves seeing students and their parents.

Moreover, students forced to pay full-cost tuition, even though repayment of the debt is spread over a lifetime of earnings, will calculate the relative advantages of alternative educational programs with some increased care. It is quite possible that there will be a shift away from the current pattern of the A.B. degree to increasing vocationalism and professionalism. The emphasis will once more be on marketable skills and the development of talent, rather than the acquisition of status.

There are a number of programs in the planning stage and several at the level of implementation which will enable students to borrow a substantial portion or all of their college tuition and repay it through an income tax or social security payroll-type deduction system. A number of these programs go beyond the field of college and university training and open up the field of government-guaranteed loans to students who wish to pursue any field of study for which they are qualified. These programs are of intense interest for those Americans concerned with educational reform because they will increase educational diversity and because they will make both the educational institution and the student responsible.

No one action or program will restore the authority of higher education in America. But unless that authority is restored, the university will drift increasingly into the orbit of petty power politics. It will be administered by time-serving men and be the prey of power brokers within the institution, bent not on achieving the educational goals of the institution but on gaining some momentary and trivial political advantage. In the final analysis, the college and the university will discover that they cannot function in the world of power, that education and coercion are incompatible, and that the price of their continued existence is a rededication to the life of the mind, the master-student relationship, and the authority in education and society which derives from these educational commonplaces.

The Lost Tools
of Learning

Dorothy L. Sayers

That I, whose experience of teaching is extremely limited, should presume to discuss education is a matter, surely, that calls for no apology. It is a kind of behavior to which the present climate of opinion is wholly favorable. Bishops air their opinions about economics; biologists, about metaphysics; inorganic chemists about theology; the most irrelevant people are appointed to highly technical ministries; and plain, blunt men write to the papers to say that Epstein and Picasso do not know how to draw. Up to a certain point, and provided that the criticisms are made with a reasonable modesty, these activities are commendable. Too much specialization is not a good thing. There is also one excellent reason why the veriest amateur may feel entitled to have an opinion about education. For if we are not all professional teachers, we have all, at some time or other, been taught. Even if we learnt nothing—perhaps in particular if we learnt nothing—our contribution to the discussion may have a potential value.

I propose to deal with the subject of teaching, properly so-called. It is in the highest degree improbable that the reforms I propose will ever be carried into effect. Neither the parents, nor the training colleges, nor the examination boards, nor the boards of governors, nor the ministries of education would countenance them for a moment. For they amount to this: that if we are to produce a society of educated people, fitted to preserve their intellectual freedom amid the complex pressures of our modern society, we must turn back the wheel of progress some four or five hundred years, to the point at which education began to lose sight of its true object, toward the end of the Middle Ages.

Before you dismiss me with the appropriate phrase —reactionary, romantic, medievalist, *laudator temporis acti,* or whatever tag comes first to hand—I will ask you to consider one or two miscellaneous questions that hang about at the back, perhaps, of all our minds, and occasionally pop out to worry us.

Disquieting Questions

When we think about the remarkably early age at which the young men went up to the university in, let us say, Tudor times, and thereafter were held fit to

assume responsibility for the conduct of their own
affairs, are we altogether comfortable about that artificial prolongation of intellectual childhood and ado-
lescence into the years of physical maturity which is so
marked in our own day? To postpone the acceptance of
responsibility to a late date brings with it a number of
psychological complications which, while they may interest the psychiatrist, are scarcely beneficial either to
the individual or to society. The stock argument in
favor of postponing the school leaving-age and pro-
longing the period of education generally is that there
is now so much more to learn than there was in the
Middle Ages. This is partly true, but not wholly. The
modern boy and girl are certainly taught more subjects
—but does that always mean that they actually know
more?

Has it ever struck you as odd, or unfortunate, that
today, when the proportion of literacy throughout
western Europe is higher than it has ever been, people
should have become susceptible to the influence of
advertisement and mass-propaganda to an extent
hitherto unheard-of and unimagined? Do you put this
down to the mere mechanical fact that the press and
the radio and so on have made propaganda much easier
to distribute over a wide area? Or do you sometimes
have an uneasy suspicion that the product of modern
educational methods is less good than he or she might
be at disentangling fact from opinion and the proven
from the plausible?

Have you ever, in listening to a debate among adult

and presumably responsible people, been fretted by the extraordinary inability of the average debater to speak to the question, or to meet and refute the arguments of speakers on the other side? Or have you ever pondered upon the extremely high incidence of irrelevant matter which crops up at committee-meetings, and upon the very great rarity of persons capable of acting as chairmen of committees? And when you think of this, and think that most of our public affairs are settled by debates and committees, have you ever felt a certain sinking of the heart?

Have you ever followed a discussion in the newspapers or elsewhere and noticed how frequently writers fail to define the terms they use? Or how often, if one man does define his terms, another will assume in his reply that he was using the terms in precisely the opposite sense to that in which he has already defined them?

Have you ever been faintly troubled by the amount of slipshod syntax going about? And if so, are you troubled because it is inelegant or because it may lead to dangerous misunderstandings?

Do you ever find that young people, when they have left school, not only forget most of what they have learnt (that is only to be expected) but forget also or betray that they have never really known, how to tackle a new subject for themselves? Are you often bothered by coming across grown-up men and women who seem unable to distinguish between a book that is sound, scholarly and properly documented, and one that is to any trained eye, very conspicuously none of these things? Or who cannot handle a library catalogue? Or who, when faced with a book of reference, betray a curious inability to extract from it the passages relevant to the particular question which interests them?

Do you often come across people for whom, all their lives, a "subject" remains a "subject," divided by watertight bulkheads from all other "subjects," so that they experience very great difficulty in making an immediate mental connection between, let us say, algebra and detective fiction, sewage disposal and the price of salmon—or, more generally, between such spheres of knowledge as philosophy and economics, or chemistry and art?

A Few Examples

Are you occasionally perturbed by the things written by adult men and women for adult men and women to read?

We find a well-known biologist writing in a weekly paper to the effect that: "It is an argument against the existence of a Creator" (I think he put it more strongly; but since I have, most unfortunately, mislaid the reference, I will put his claim at its lowest) "an argument against the existence of a Creator that the same kind of variations which are produced by natural selection can be produced at will by stockbreeders." One might feel tempted to say that it is rather an argument *for* the existence of a Creator. Actually, of course, it is neither: all it proves is that the same material causes (recombination of the chromosomes by crossbreeding and so forth) are sufficient to account for all observed variations—just as the various combinations of the same thirteen semitones are materially sufficient to account for Beethoven's *Moonlight Sonata* and the noise the cat makes by walking on the keys. But the cat's performance neither proves nor disproves the existence of Beethoven; and all that is proved by the biologist's argument is that he was unable to distinguish between a material and a final cause.

Here is a sentence from no less academic a source than a front-page article in the [London] *Times Literary Supplement:*

> The Frenchman, Alfred Epinas, pointed out that certain species (e.g., ants and wasps) can only face the horrors of life and death in association.

I do not know what the Frenchman actually did say: what the Englishman says he said is patently meaningless. We cannot know whether life holds any horror for the ant, nor in what sense the isolated wasp which you kill upon the windowpane can be said to "face" or not to "face" the horrors of death. The subject of the article is mass-behavior in *man;* and the human motives have been unobtrusively transferred from the main proposition to the supporting instance. Thus the argument, in effect, assumes what it sets out to prove—a fact which would become immediately apparent if it were presented in a formal syllogism. This is only a small and haphazard example of a vice which pervades whole books—particularly books written by men of science on metaphysical subjects.

Another quotation from the same issue of the *T.L.S.* comes in fittingly here to wind up this random collection of disquieting thoughts—this time from a review of Sir Richard Livingstone's *Some Tasks for Education:*

> More than once the reader is reminded of the value of an intensive study of at least one subject, so as to learn "the meaning of knowledge" and what precision and persistence is needed to attain it. Yet there is elsewhere full recognition of the distressing fact that a man may be master in one field and show no better judgment than his neighbor anywhere else; he remembers what he has learnt, but forgets altogether how he learned it.

I would draw your attention particularly to that last sentence, which offers an explanation of what the writer rightly calls the "distressing fact" that the intellectual skills bestowed upon us by our education are not readily transferable to subjects other than those in which we acquired them: "he remembers what he has learnt, but forgets altogether how he learned it."

The Art of Learning

Is not the great defect of our education today—a defect traceable through all the disquieting symptoms of trouble that I have mentioned—that although we often succeed in teaching our pupils "subjects," we fail lamentably on the whole in teaching them how to think: They learn everything, except the art of learning. It is as though we had taught a child, mechanically and by rule of thumb, to play "The Harmonious Blacksmith" upon the piano, but had never taught him the scale or how to read music; so that, having memorized "The Harmonious Blacksmith," he still had not the faintest notion how to proceed from that to tackle "The Last Rose of Summer." Why do I say, "As though"? In certain of the arts and crafts we sometimes do precisely this—requiring a child to "express himself" in paint before we teach him how to handle the colors and the brush. There is a school of thought which believes this to be the right way to set about the job. But observe—it is not the way in which a trained craftsman will go about to teach himself a new medium. He, having learned by experience the best way to economize labor and take the thing by the right end, will start off by doodling about on an odd piece of material, in order to "give himself the feel of the tool."

Let us now look at the medieval scheme of education—the syllabus of the schools. It does not matter, for the moment, whether it was devised for small children or for older students; or how long people were supposed to take over it. What matters is the light it throws upon what the men of the Middle Ages supposed to be the object and the right order of the educative process.

The Medieval Syllabus

The syllabus was divided into two parts: the Trivium and Quadrivium. The second part—the Quadrivium—consisted of "subjects," and need not for the moment concern us. The interesting thing for us is the composition of the Trivium, which preceded the Quadrivium and was the preliminary discipline for it. It consisted of three parts: Grammar, Dialectic, and Rhetoric, in that order.

Now the first thing we notice is that two at any rate of these "subjects" are not what we should call "subjects" at all: they are only methods of dealing with subjects. Grammar, indeed, is a "subject" in the sense that it does mean definitely learning a language—at that period it meant learning Latin. But language itself is simply the medium in which thought is expressed. The whole of the Trivium was, in fact, intended to teach the pupil the proper use of the tools of learning, before he began to apply them to "subjects" at all. First, he learned a language; not just how to order a meal in a foreign language, but the structure of language—*a* language, and hence of language itself—what it was, how it was put together and how it worked. Secondly, he learned how to use language: how to define his terms and make accurate statements; how to construct an argument and how to detect fallacies in argument (his own arguments and other people's). Dialectic, that is to say, embraced Logic and Disputation. Thirdly, he learned to express himself in language; how to say what he had to say elegantly and persuasively.

At the end of his course, he was required to compose a thesis upon some theme set by his masters or chosen by himself, and afterward to defend his thesis against the criticism of the faculty. By this time he would have learned—or woe betide him—not merely to write an essay on paper, but to speak audibly and intelligibly from a platform, and to use his wits quickly when heckled. There would also be questions, cogent and shrewd, from those who had already run the gantlet of debate.

It is, of course, quite true that bits and pieces of the medieval tradition still linger, or have been revived, in the ordinary school syllabus of today. Some knowledge of grammar is still required when learning a foreign language—perhaps I should say, "is again required"; for during my own lifetime we passed through a phase when the teaching of declensions and conjugations was considered rather reprehensible, and it was considered better to pick these things up as we

went along. School debating societies flourish, essays
are written; the necessity for "self-expression" is
stressed, and perhaps even overstressed. But these activities are cultivated more or less in detachment, as
belonging to the special subjects in which they are
pigeon-holed rather than as forming one coherent
scheme of mental training to which all "subjects" stand
in a subordinate relation. "Grammar" belongs especially to the "subject" of foreign languages, and essay-
writing to the "subject" called "English"; while
Dialectic has become almost entirely divorced from the
rest of the curriculum, and is frequently practiced un-
systematically and out of school-hours as a separate
exercise, only very loosely related to the main business
of learning. Taken by and large, the great difference of
emphasis between the two conceptions holds good:
modern education concentrates on *teaching subjects,*
leaving the method of thinking, arguing and expressing
one's conclusions to be picked up by the scholar as he
goes along; medieval education concentrated on first
forging and learning to handle the tools of learning,
using whatever subject came handy as a piece of material on which to doodle until the use of the tool became second nature.

"Subjects" of some kind there must be, of course.
One cannot learn the theory of grammar without learning an actual language, or learn to argue and orate
without speaking about something in particular. The
debating subjects of the Middle Ages were drawn

largely from Theology, or from the Ethics and History of Antiquity. Often, indeed, they became stereotyped, especially toward the end of the period, and the farfetched and wire-drawn absurdities of scholastic argument fretted Milton and provide food for merriment even to this day. Whether they were in themselves any more hackneyed and trivial than the usual subjects set nowadays for "essay-writing" I should not like to say: we may ourselves grow a little weary of "A Day in My Holidays," and all the rest of it. But most of the merriment is misplaced, because the aim and object of the debating thesis has by now been lost sight of.

Angels on a Needle

A glib speaker in the Brains Trust once entertained his audience (and reduced the late Charles Williams to helpless rage) by asserting that in the Middle Ages it was a matter of faith to know how many archangels could dance on the point of a needle. I need not say, I hope, that it never was a "matter of faith"; it was simply a debating exercise, whose set subject was the nature of angelic substance: were angels material, and if so, did they occupy space? The answer usually adjudged correct is, I believe, that angels are pure intelligencies; not material, but limited, so that they may have location in space but not extension. An analogy might be drawn from human thought, which is similarly non-material and similarly limited. Thus, if your thought is concentrated upon one thing—say, the point of a needle—it is located there in the sense that it is not elsewhere; but although it is "there," it occupies no space there, and there is nothing to prevent an infinite number of different people's thoughts being concentrated upon the same needle-point at the same time. The proper *subject* of the argument is thus seen to be the distinction between location and extension in space; the *matter* on which the argument is exercised happens to be the nature of angels (although, as we have seen, it might equally well have been something else); the practical lesson to be drawn from the argument is not to use words like "there" in a loose and unscientific way, without specifying whether you mean "located there" or "occupying space there."

Scorn in plenty has been poured out upon the medieval passion for hair-splitting: but when we look at the shameless abuse made, in print and on the platform, of controversial expressions with shifting and ambiguous connotations, we may feel it in our hearts to wish that every reader and hearer had been so defensively armored by his education as to be able to cry: *Distinguo*.

Unarmed

For we let our young men and women go out unarmed, in a day when armor was never so necessary. *By teaching them all to read, we have left them at the mercy of the printed word.* By the invention of the film and the radio, we have made certain that no aversion to reading shall secure them from the incessant battery of words, words, words. They do not know what the words mean; they do not know how to ward them off or blunt their edge or fling them back; they are a prey to words in their emotions instead of being the masters of them in their intellects. We who were scandalized in 1940 when men were sent to fight armored tanks with rifles, are not scandalized when young men and women are sent into the world to fight massed propaganda with a smattering of "subjects"; and when whole classes and whole nations become hypnotized by the arts of the spellbinder, we have the impudence to be astonished. We dole out lip-service to the importance of education—lip-service and, just occasionally, a little grant of money; we postpone the school leaving-age, and plan to build bigger and better schools; the teachers slave conscientiously in and out of school-hours; and yet, as I believe, all this devoted effort is largely frustrated, because we have lost the tools of learning, and in their absence can only make a botched and piece-meal job of it.

What, then, are we to do? We cannot go back to the Middle Ages. That is a cry to which we have become accustomed. We cannot go back—or can we? *Distinguo.* I should like every term in the proposition defined. Does "Go back" mean a retrogression in time, or the revision of an error? The first is clearly impossible *per se;* the second is a thing which wise men do every day. Obviously the twentieth century is not and cannot be the fourteenth; but if "the Middle Ages" is, in this context, simply a picturesque phrase denoting a particular educational theory, there seems to be no *a priori* reason why we should not "go back" to it—with modifications—as we have already "gone back" with modifications, to, let us say, the idea of playing Shakespeare's plays as he wrote them, and not in the "modernized" versions of Cibber and Garrick, which once seemed to be the latest thing in theatrical progress.

Let us amuse ourselves by imagining that such progressive retrogression is possible. Let us make a clean sweep of all educational authorities, and furnish ourselves with a nice little school of boys and girls, whom we may experimentally equip for the intellectual conflict along lines chosen by ourselves. We will endow them with exceptionally docile parents; we will staff our school with teachers who are themselves perfectly familiar with the aims and methods of the Trivium; we will have our buildings and staff large enough to allow our classes to be small enough for adequate handling; and we will postulate a Board of Examiners willing and qualified to test the products we turn out. Thus prepared, we will attempt to sketch out a syllabus—a modern Trivium "with modifications"; and we will see where we get to.

But first: what age shall the children be? Well, if one is to educate them on novel lines, it will be better that they should have nothing to unlearn; besides, one cannot begin a good thing too early, and the Trivium is by its nature not learning, but a preparation for learning. We will, therefore, *"catch 'em young,"* requiring only of our pupils that they shall be able to read, write and cipher.

The Three Ages

My views about child-psychology are, I admit, neither orthodox nor enlightened. Looking back upon myself (since I am the child I know best and the only child I can pretend to know from inside) I recognize *three states of development.* These, in a rough-and-ready fashion, I will call the Poll-Parrot, the Pert, and the Poetic—the last coinciding, approximately, with the onset of puberty. The *Poll-Parrot stage* is the one in which learning by heart is easy and, on the whole, pleasurable; whereas reasoning is difficult and, on the whole, little relished. At this age, one readily memorizes the shapes and appearances of things; one likes to recite the number-plates of cars; one rejoices in the chanting of rhymes and the rumble and thunder of unintelligible polysyllables; one enjoys the mere accumulation of things. The *Pert Age,* which follows upon this (and naturally, overlaps it to some extent), is characterized by contradicting, answering-back, liking to "catch people out" (especially one's elders) and in the propounding of conundrums. Its nuisance-value is extremely high. *It usually sets in about the eighth grade.* The Poetic Age is popularly known as the "difficult" age. It is self-centered; it yearns to express itself; it rather specializes in being misunderstood; it is restless and tries to achieve independence; and, with good luck and good guidance, it should show the beginnings of creativeness, a reaching-out toward a synthesis of what it already knows, and a deliberate eagerness to know and do some one thing in preference to all others. Now it seems to me that the layout of the Trivium adapts itself with a singular appropriateness to these three ages: Grammar to the Poll-Parrot, Dialectic to the Pert, and Rhetoric to the Poetic Age.

Let us begin, then, with *Grammar*. This, in practice, means the grammar of some language in particular; and it must be an inflected language. The grammatical structure of an uninflected language is far too analytical to be tackled by any one without previous practice in Dialectic. Moreover, the inflected languages interpret the uninflected, whereas the uninflected are of little use in interpreting the inflected. *I will say at once, quite firmly, that the best grounding for education is the Latin grammar.* I say this, not because Latin is traditional and medieval, but simply because even a rudimentary knowledge of Latin cuts down the labor and pains of learning almost any other subject by at least fifty percent. It is the key to the vocabulary and structure of all the Romance languages and to the structure of all the Teutonic languages, as well as to the technical vocabulary of all the sciences and to the literature of the entire Mediterranean civilization, together with all its historical documents.

Those whose pedantic preference for a living language persuades them to deprive their pupils of all these advantages might substitute Russian, whose grammar is still more primitive. Russian is, of course, helpful with the other Slav dialects. There is something also to be said for Classical Greek. But my own choice is Latin. Having thus pleased the Classicists among you, I will proceed to horrify them by adding that I do not think it either wise or necessary to cramp the ordinary pupil upon the Procrustean bed of the Augustan Age, with its highly elaborate and artificial verse-forms and oratory.

Latin should be begun as early as possible—at a time when inflected speech seems no more astonishing than any other phenomenon in an astonishing world; and when the chanting of *"Amo, Amas, Amat"* is as ritually agreeable to the feelings as the chanting of "eeny, meeny, miney, mo."

During this age we must, of course, exercise the mind on other things beside Latin grammar. Observation and memory are the faculties most lively at this period; and if we are to learn a contemporary foreign language we should begin now, before the facial and mental muscles become rebellious to strange intonations. Spoken French or German can be practiced alongside the grammatical discipline of the Latin.

The Use of Memory

In English, verse and prose can be learned by heart, and the pupil's memory should be stored with stories of every kind—classical myth, European legend, and so forth. I do not think that the classical stories and masterpieces of ancient literature should be made the vile bodies on which to practice the technics of Grammar—that was a fault of medieval education which we need not perpetuate. The stories can be enjoyed and remembered in English, and related to their origin at a subsequent stage. Recitation aloud should be practiced—individually or in chorus; for we must not forget that we are laying the groundwork for Disputation and Rhetoric.

The grammar of History should consist, I think, of dates, events, anecdotes and personalities. A set of dates to which one can peg all later historical knowledge is of enormous help later on in establishing the perspective of history. It does not greatly matter which dates: those of the Kings of England will do very nicely, provided that they are accompanied by pictures of costumes, architecture, and other "everyday things," so that the mere mention of a date calls up a strong visual presentment of the whole period.

Geography will similarly be presented in its factual aspect, with maps, natural features and visual presentment of customs, costumes, flora, fauna and so on; and I believe myself that the discredited and old-fashioned memorizing of a few capital cities, rivers, mountain ranges, etc., does no harm. Stamp-collecting may be encouraged.

Science, in the Poll-Parrot period, arranges itself naturally and easily round collections—the identifying and naming of specimens and, in general, the kind of thing that used to be called "natural history," or, still more charmingly, "natural philosophy." To know the names and properties of things is, at this age, a satisfaction in itself; to recognize a devil's coach-horse at sight, and assure one's foolish elders that, in spite of its appearance, it does not sting; to be able to pick out Cassiopeia and the Pleiades; to be aware that a whale is not a fish, and a bat not a bird—all these things give a pleasant sensation of superiority; while to know a rinksnake from an adder or a poisonous from an edible toadstool is a kind of knowledge that has also a practical value.

The grammar of Mathematics begins, of course, with the multiplication table, which, if not learnt now will never be learnt with pleasure; and with the recognition of geometrical shapes and the grouping of numbers. These exercises lead naturally to the doing of simple sums in arithmetic; and if the pupil shows a bent that way, a facility acquired at this stage is all to the good. More complicated mathematical processes may, and perhaps should, be postponed, for reasons which will presently appear.

So far (except, of course, for the Latin), our curriculum contains nothing that departs very far from common practice. The difference will be felt rather in *the attitude of the teachers, who must look upon all these activities less as "subjects" in themselves than as a gathering-together of material for use in the next part of the Trivium.* What that material actually is, is only of secondary importance; *but it is as well that anything and everything which can usefully be committed to memory should be memorized at this period, whether it is immediately intelligible or not. The modern tendency is to try and force rational explanations on a child's mind at too early an age.* Intelligent questions, spontaneously asked, should, of course, receive an immediate and rational answer; but it is a great mistake to suppose that a child cannot readily enjoy and remember things that are beyond its power to analyze— particularly if those things have a strong imaginative appeal, an attractive jingle, or an abundance of rich, resounding polysyllables.

The Mistress-Science

This reminds me of *the grammar of Theology.* I shall add it to the curriculum, because Theology is the mistress-science, without which the whole educational structure will necessarily lack its final synthesis. Those who disagree about this will remain content to leave their pupils' education still full of loose ends. This will matter rather less than it might, since by the time that the tools of learning have been forged the student will be able to tackle Theology for himself, and will probably insist upon doing so and making sense of it. Still, it is as well to have this matter also handy and ready for the reason to work upon. At the grammatical age, therefore, we should become acquainted with the story of God and Man in outline—*i.e.,* the Old and New Testament presented as parts of a single narrative of Creation, Rebellion and Redemption—and also with "the Creed, the Lord's Prayer and the Ten Commandments." At this stage, it does not matter nearly so much that these things should be fully understood as that they should be known and remembered.

It is difficult to say at what age, precisely, we should pass from the first to *the second part of the Trivium.* Generally speaking, the answer is: so soon as the pupil shows himself disposed to pertness and interminable argument. For as, in the first part, the master-facilities are Observation and Memory, so in the second, the master-faculty is the Discursive Reason. In the first, the exercise to which the rest of the material was, as it were, keyed, was the Latin grammar; in the second, the key-exercise will be *Formal Logic.* It is here that our curriculum shows its first sharp divergence from modern standards. The disrepute into which Formal Logic has fallen is entirely unjustified; and its neglect is the root cause of nearly all those disquieting symptoms which we have noted in the modern intellectual constitution.

A secondary cause for the disfavor into which Formal Logic has fallen is the belief that it is entirely based upon universal assumptions that are either unprovable or tautological. This is not true. Not all universal propositions are of this kind. But even if they were, it would make no difference, since every syllogism whose major premise is in the form "All A is B" can be recast in hypothetical form. Logic is the art of arguing correctly: "If A, then B": the method is not invalidated by the hypothetical character of A. Indeed, the practical utility of Formal Logic today lies not so much in the establishment of positive conclusions as in the prompt detection and exposure of invalid inference.

Relation to Dialectic

Let us now quickly review our material and see how it is to be related to Dialectic. On *the Language side*, we shall now have our Vocabulary and Morphology at our fingertips; henceforward *we can concentrate more particularly on Syntax and Analysis* (*i.e.*, the logical construction of speech) and the history of Language (*i.e.*, how we come to arrange our speech as we do in order to convey our thoughts).

Our *Reading* will proceed from narrative and lyric to essays, argument and criticism, and the pupil will learn to try his own hand at writing this kind of thing. Many lessons—on whatever subject—will take the form of debates; and the place of individual or choral recitation will be taken by dramatic performances, with special attention to plays in which an argument is stated in dramatic form.

Mathematics—Algebra, Geometry, and the more advanced kind of Arithmetic—will now enter into the syllabus and take its place as what it really is: not a separate "subject" but a *subdepartment of Logic*. It is neither more nor less than the rule of the syllogism in its particular application to number and measurement, and should be taught as such, instead of being, for some, a dark mystery, and for others, a special revelation, neither illuminating nor illuminated by any other part of knowledge.

History, aided by a simple system of ethics derived from the grammar of Theology, will provide much suitable material for discussion: Was the behavior of this statesman justified? What was the effect of such an enactment? What are the arguments for and against this or that form of government? We shall thus get an introduction to Constitutional History—a subject meaningless to the young child, but of absorbing interest to those who are prepared to argue and debate. *Theology* itself will furnish material for argument about conduct and morals; and should have its scope extended by a simplified course of dogmatic theology (*i.e.,* the rational structure of Christian thought), clarifying the relations between the dogma and the ethics, and lending itself to that application of ethical principles in particular instances which is properly called casuistry. *Geography* and the *Sciences* will all likewise provide material for Dialectic.

The World Around Us

But above all, we must not neglect the material which is so abundant in the pupils' own daily life.

There is a delightful passage in Leslie Paul's *The Living Hedge* which tells how a number of small boys enjoyed themselves for days arguing about an extraordinary shower of rain which had fallen in their town—a shower so localized that it left one-half of the main street wet and the other dry. Could one, they argued, properly say that it had rained that day *on* or *over* the town or only *in* the town? How many drops of water were required to constitute rain? and so on. Argument about this led on to a host of similar problems about rest and motion, sleep and waking, *est* and *non est,* and the infinitesimal division of time. The whole passage is an admirable example of the spontaneous development of the ratiocinative faculty and the natural and proper thirst of the awakening reason for definition of terms and exactness of statement. All events are food for such an appetite.

An umpire's decision; the degree to which one may transgress the spirit of a regulation without being trapped by the letter; on such questions as these, children are born casuists, and their natural propensity only needs to be developed and trained—and, especially, brought into an intelligible relationship with events in the grown-up world. The newspapers are full of good material for such exercises: legal decisions, on the one hand, in cases where the cause at issue is not too abstruse; on the other, fallacious reasoning and muddleheaded argument, with which the correspondence columns of certain papers one could name are abundantly stocked.

"Pert Age" Criticism

Wherever the matter for Dialectic is found, it is, of course, highly important that attention should be focused upon the beauty and economy of a fine demonstration or a well-turned argument, lest veneration should wholly die. Criticism must not be merely destructive; though at the same time both teacher and pupils must be ready to detect fallacy, slipshod reasoning, ambiguity, irrelevance and redundancy, and to pounce upon them like rats.

This is the moment when precis-writing may be usefully undertaken; together with such exercises as the writing of an essay, and the reduction of it, when written, by 25 or 50 percent.

It will, doubtless, be objected that to encourage young persons at the Pert Age to brow-beat, correct

and argue with their elders will render them perfectly
intolerable. My answer is that children of that age are
intolerable anyhow; and that their natural argumenta-
tiveness may just as well be canalized to good purpose
as allowed to run away into the sands. It may, indeed,
be rather less obtrusive at home if it is disciplined in
school; and, anyhow, elders who have abandoned the
wholesome principle that children should be seen and
not heard have no one to blame but themselves.

Once again: the contents of the syllabus at this stage
may be anything you like. The "subjects" supply material; but they are all to be regarded as mere grist for
the mental mill to work upon. The pupils should be
encouraged to go and forage for their own information, and so guided toward the proper use of libraries
and books of reference, and shown how to tell which
sources are authoritative and which are not.

Imagination

Toward the close of this stage, the pupils will probably be beginning to discover for themselvees that their
knowledge and experience are insufficient, and that
their trained intelligences need a great deal more material to chew upon. The imagination—usually dor-
mant during the Pert Age—will reawaken, and prompt
them to suspect the limitations of logic and reason.
This means that they are passing into the Poetic Age

and are ready to embark on the study of *Rhetoric*. The doors of the storehouse of knowledge should now be thrown open for them to browse about as they will. The things once learned by rote will be seen in new contexts; the things once coldly analyzed can now be brought together to form a new synthesis; here and there a sudden insight will bring about that most exciting of all discoveries: the realization that a truism is true.

The Study of Rhetoric

It is difficult to map out any general syllabus for the study of Rhetoric: a certain freedom is demanded. *In literature, appreciation should be again allowed to take the lead over destructive criticism;* and self-expression in writing can go forward, with its tools now sharpened to cut clean and observe proportion. Any child that already shows a disposition to specialize should be given his head: for, when the use of the tools has been well and truly learned it is available for any study whatever. It would be well, I think, that each pupil should learn to do one, or two, subjects really well, while taking a few classes in subsidiary subjects so as to keep his mind open to the interrelations of all knowledge. Indeed, at this stage, our difficulty will be to keep "subjects" apart; *for a Dialectic will have shown all branches of learning to be interrelated, so*

Rhetoric will tend to show that all knowledge is one. To show this, and show why it is so, is preeminently the task of the Mistress-science. But whether Theology is studied or not, we should at least insist that children who seem inclined to specialize on the mathematical and scientific side should be obliged to attend some lessons in the Humanities and *vice versa.* At this stage also, the Latin grammar, having done its work, may be dropped for those who prefer to carry on their language studies on the modern side; while those who are likely never to have any great use or aptitude for mathematics might also be allowed to rest, more or less, upon their oars. Generally speaking: whatsoever is *mere* apparatus may now be allowed to fall into the background, while the trained mind is gradually prepared for specialization in the "subjects" which, when the Trivium is completed, it should be perfectly well equipped to tackle on its own. The final synthesis of the Trivium—the presentation and public defense of the thesis—should be restored in some form; perhaps as a kind of "leaving examination" during the last term at school.

The scope of Rhetoric depends also on whether the pupil is to be turned out into the world at the age of 16 or whether he is to proceed to the university. Since, really, Rhetoric should be taken at about 14, the first category of pupil should study Grammar from about 9 to 11, and Dialectic from 12 to 14; his last two school years would then be devoted to Rhetoric, which, in his case, would be of a fairly specialized and vocational kind, suiting him to enter immediately upon some practical career. A pupil of the second category would finish his Dialectical course in his Preparatory School, and take Rhetoric during his first two years at his Public School. At 16, he would be ready to start upon those "subjects" which are proposed for his later study at the university; and this part of the education will correspond to the medieval Quadrivium. *What this amounts to is that the ordinary pupil, whose formal education ends at 16, will take the Trivium only; whereas scholars will take both Trivium and Quadrivium.*

The University at Sixteen?

Is the Trivium, then, a sufficient education for life? Properly taught, I believe that it should be. At the end of the Dialectic, the children will probably seem to be far behind their coevals brought up on old-fashioned "modern" methods, so far as detailed knowledge of specific subjects is concerned. But after the age of 14 they should be able to overhaul the others hand over fist. Indeed, I am not at all sure that a pupil thoroughly proficient in the Trivium would not be fit to proceed immediately to the university at the age of 16, thus proving himself the equal of his medieval counterpart, whose precocity astonished us at the beginning of this discussion. *This, to be sure, would make hay of the English public-school system, and disconcert the universities very much.* It would, for example, make quite a different thing of the Oxford and Cambridge boat-race.

But I am not here to consider the feelings of academic bodies: I am concerned only with the proper training of the mind to encounter and deal with the formidable mass of undigested problems presented to it by the modern world. For the tools of learning are the same, in any and every subject; and the person who knows how to use them will, at any age, get the mastery of a new subject in half the time and with a quarter of the effort expended by the person who has not the tools at his command. To learn six subjects without remembering how they were learnt does nothing to ease the approach to a seventh; *to have learnt and remembered the art of learning makes the approach to every subject an open door.*

Educational Capital Depleted

Before concluding these necessarily very sketchy suggestions, I ought to say why I think it necessary, in these days, to go back to a discipline which we had discarded. The truth is that for the last 300 years or so we have been living upon our educational capital. The post-Renaissance world, bewildered and excited by the profusion of new "subjects" offered to it, broke away from the old discipline (which had, indeed, become sadly dull and stereotyped in its practical application) and imagined that henceforth it could, as it were, disport itself happily in its new and extended Quadrivium without passing through the Trivium. But the scholastic tradition, though broken and maimed, still lingered in the public schools and universities: Milton, however much he protested against it, was formed by it—the debate of the Fallen Angels, and the disputation of Abdiel with Satan have the toolmarks of the Schools upon them, and might, incidentally, profitably figure as set passages for our Dialectical studies. Right down to the nineteenth century, our public affairs were mostly managed, and our books and journals were for the most part written, by people brought up in homes, and trained in places, where that tradition was still alive in the memory and almost in the blood. Just so, many people today who are atheist or agnostic in religion, are governed in their conduct by a code of Christian ethics which is so rooted in their unconscious assumptions that it never occurs to them to question it.

Forgotten Roots

But one cannot live on capital forever. A tradition, however firmly rooted, if it is never watered, though it dies hard, yet in the end it dies. *And today a great num-*

ber—*perhaps the majority*—of the men and women who handle our affairs, write our books and our newspapers, carry out research, present our plays and our films, speak from our platforms and pulpits—yes, and *who educate our young people, have never, even in a lingering traditional memory, undergone the scholastic discipline.* Less and less do the children who come to be educated bring any of that tradition with them. We have lost the tools of learning—the axe and the wedge, the hammer and the saw, the chisel and the plane—that were so adaptable to all tasks. Instead of them, we have merely a set of complicated jigs, each of which will do but one task and no more, and in using which eye and hand receive no training, so that no man ever sees the work as a whole or "looks to the end of the work."

What use is it to pile task on task and prolong the days of labor, if at the close the chief object is left unattained? It is not the fault of the teachers—they work only too hard already. *The combined folly of a civilization that has forgotten its own roots is forcing them to shore up the tottering weight of an educational structure that is built upon sand.* They are doing for their pupils the work which the pupils themselves ought to do. *For the sole true end of education is simply this: to teach men how to learn for themselves; and whatever instruction fails to do this is effort spent in vain.*

Index

This book was Linotype set in the Times Roman series of type. The face was designed by Stanley Morison to be used in the news columns of the *Times* of London. The *Times* was seeking a typeface that would be condensed enough to accommodate a substantial number of words per column without sacrificing readability and still have an attractive, contemporary appearance. This design was an immediate success. It is used in many periodicals throughout the world and is one of the most popular textfaces presently in use for book work.

Printed on paper that is acid-free and meets the requirements of the American National Standard for Permanence of Paper for Printed Library Materials, Z39.48-1992. ∞

Book design by Design Center, Inc., Indianapolis, Indiana
Typography by Weimer Typesetting Co., Inc., Indianapolis, Indiana
Printed by Worzalla Publishing Co., Stevens Point, Wisconsin